To Ralph,

On the occasion of your retirement from Eagle Star on 28th April, 1995. With best wishes the future.

from
Harold.

ARRIVAL PRESS

VETERANS OF VICTORY

Edited

By

SUZY GOODALL

First published in Great Britain in 1995 by
ARRIVAL PRESS
1 - 2 Wainman Road, Woodston,
Peterborough, PE2 7BU

HB ISBN 1 85786 273 2
SB ISBN1 85786 278 3

Foreword

All the poets included in this anthology
have shared the same experience - that of
the horrors of the Second World War. I'm
sure that without being there, like myself, it
would be difficult to imagine the trauma
and pain that war can bring.

The poems included in *Veterans of
Victory* will give you a little understanding
into the thoughts and feelings of all those
involved - from the rations to the air raids
and the soldiers to the families left at
home - each poet giving you an insight
into the death, destruction and power that
war had upon the world.

Suzy Goodall
Editor

CONTENTS

FALSE GLORY

I came across the enemy
He was hiding in the dirt
All the weeks of training
Could not postpone this hurt
As he laid down his weapons
I felt a surge of tears
That I a human being
Could perpetrate such fears
I lifted up my rifle
Drew it level with my eye
And suddenly it dawned on me
This man was about to die
They trained me to be capable
To take away a life
But then I found myself wondering
What if he has a wife?
I brought back down my weapon
Saw his look of surprise
I thought of the promise of glory
And reality proved it a lie.

Susan Pettit

MEMORIES OF DEN-BOSCH OCT 44

We went into the City at dead of night
Were well established before daylight
House to house we cleared off bosch
To free the City of S-Hertogenbosch,
Buildings across the square to take
We crouched along the old lock gate,

I dashed across with men to follow
When I came to I laid in a hollow,
The blood was pouring from my head and side
I had been left for dead but had not died,
Shells were bursting all around
As I outstretched upon the ground,

Guns were firing but I could not hear
I said a prayer and had no fear,
I crawled along a terraced street
And tried my best to get on my feet,
A door was opened then slammed shut
So I crawled away among the dust,

I reached an opening further back
And there my men with prisoners from attack,
Years later when I returned
The house I sought it had burned,
The place had changed was clear and bright
As I stood in silence in broad daylight,
My thoughts went back to 44
And all those men who are no more,

Mike Hannon

NEVER AGAIN

They returned again to the beaches
Where they'd all been once before
Standing there in the sunshine
Had there really been a war.

But their thoughts were not on the present
As they gazed far out to sea
And they saw once again the invasion
That was vivid in their memory.

Then they glanced at the stone clad memorial
And the names of the units they knew
They remembered their comrades in battle
And the men who had never come through.

They saw the cemeteries nearby
The crosses in rows standing there
And with tears in their eyes they remembered
Those who still had crosses to bear.

It's fifty long years since they landed
And the boys have all turned to old men
But one thought in their minds keep them going
We must not let it happen again.

R C L Smith

NORMANDY HYMN

When bombs and shells were bursting
And ships on billows roll
A skylark was ascending -
God still was in control.

Let's not forget our Comrades
Enduring bitter pain
Who waded in so valiant
Did not return again.

How calm today the beaches
Where once the bullets flew
And Caen was dark with fighting;
The sky is peaceful blue.

Oh give us faith and wisdom
To life a sweeter taste
And teach reluctant nations
That war is still a waste.

And from thy heavenly splendour
Let war and hatred cease
With love and fervent praying,
That lead to lasting peace.

J T Roberts

WHAT PRICE VICTORY?

'What did you do in the war, Dad?'
The little boy enquired.
His father took him by the hand
He suddenly looked tired.
'I lost so many friends, son,
I lost a brother too,
A happy lad of seventeen
With eyes of china blue.
We may have won the victory,
But still the cost was dear,
And many friends are missing
Who should be round us, here;
And though its all been quiet
This past ten years or so,
There's trouble round the corner
And I might have to go.
Somebody has to lose, lad,
Just read your history,
And say a prayer for those men
Who won the victory.'

C A Lee

THOUGHTS FROM THE HEART AND THE TRENCHES

O, this war has put great hindrance on me.
It's heightened my fight for living alright, and magnified my
                                          hostility!

We are not machines waiting ahead -
Only men with heavy boots like lead!
Fighting I am, for my country and my wife,
Not to be left to defend for herself - if I lose my life!
I don't want another man to fill these size eight boots,
I'm praying to live to go back to my roots.

We are not illusions but flesh and blood men, mad frantic men,
Carrying our Toms, Dicks and Harrys! Wounded, dead, some never
                                          married
No fruits of life for those poor souls who never tallied.
Mothers' baby boys, shot down in their prime by a gerry,
They didn't get their fair bite of life's sweet cherry!

Brave men . . . *brave*! We never had the choice,
What would have happened if we said war, no thank you! In a girlie
                                          voice.
For we are men! Not mamby pambies tied to our mother's apron
                                          strings.
Men big enough, to fight for our King!
Handsome action men,
The type romantic women write about with pen,
I watch a few die
Like stars blacked out of the sky.
Sometimes in the darkness of night,
I lay and wonder if my youthful face will once again see the light!

My life's on ration dreaming of lost passion -
I've yet to bounce my baby on my knee
Tell him or her, a story of pirates and golden haired mermaids
                                          that live in the sea.
O, my Kate keep the home fire burning, -
For it is your love I am yearning!

I've become languid and cold . . .
This mud blanket has taken hold.
I'm sticking it out! . . .
But what the hell is this war all about?
I want my woman around me - not a wreath!
So, I'm waiting for you Hitler! . . . At the drop of a handkerchief!

Joy Burton-Phillips

NATIONAL FIRE SERVICE

Sirens wailing,
Fire bells ringing,
London's burning,
Planes are droning.
Bombs are dropping,
Fires are raging.
Hoses playing
On flames leaping,
In the Control Room
Firewomen plotting -
Movements of vehicles
That are attending.
The dawn at last, is breaking,
Eyes that are tired and aching,
We try to get a little rest
Before we're called
To do our best,
To win this war, and peace at last.

Trixie Heveron

THE END

The cold wet rain, night as dark as death
And the way unknown.
Steps that drag and ache, reaching no goal
But adding new horrors.

No voice, no grunt or squeak from nature
A drip drop drip from sodden leaves
And the rustle of rain.

Sink down into slime and weep upon wetness
Strive no more for this is infinite night
God giving sky and sun and warm earth
Has seen it gored with guns and blood
God's tears flood earth and man
And all is sea.

Blast and rent tall cities
Scream for death and ply naked blade
Still there is life.
Cons of time have drowned the noise of battle
Trivial eruption weighs little upon the course of ages.
So lay down gun and sword and bring out harp.
Let voices ring with song and not with fear
Lapse into idleness and drunken foolishness
But speak no more of fighting.
Fine deeds and thoughts will spring from sagas well enough.

V L Bagley

UNTITLED

How far away and yet so near
Those wartime days seem now
Wrinkles on my once smooth cheeks
Furrows on my brow.
And yet inside I'm still nineteen
The years between might not have been.
Memories come flooding back
When someone mentions the *ack-ack*.
Manning duties by the score -
Cookhouse, guard, latrines and more.
Often up before the lark
Frozen fingered in the dark.
Nissen huts, tents and *spider* blocks
A far, far cry from home
I sometimes wonder briefly
What made me want to roam.
But how glad I am that I did so
For many friends I got to know,
And whilst we went our separate ways
I still recall those other days.
A few of us have kept in touch
Through all the passing years
And shared our good news and the bad
The happiness and tears.
The word gets spread when one of us
Departs our earthly home
For years roll on and sadly
We have to say adieu.
But glad we met and always friend
I will remember you.

Kathleen Jarrold

WOMAN AT WAR

We all lined up tin hat in hand,
Khaki knickers and shirt,
A few tears shed we had to go
Something we could not shirk,
Rise at six creep to the loo
A wash then out on the square,
The sergeant's voice like a blooming gun,
Laugh we did not dare,
We were put on the guns,
Called out at night,
All muffed up to our eyes,
Curlers hidden under our hat
Running about like flies.
This went on for six long years,
Yawl when will it end,
My bloke is waiting to marry me
The country I must defend
At last D Day came
Off with the Khaki shirt
Out to celebrate my wedding day
To my beloved Bert.

Thelma Hymes

THINGS I WILL CHERISH

When peace comes to the world again,
And I return once more
We shall build our lives anew,
But not quite as before
Things we took for granted,
I'll be thankful for each day,
Freedom, home, the things for which,
We now must fight and pray

I did not know, until I went,
How much you meant to me
Your love, your dear companionship.
Your help and sympathy
When together once again,
We make another start.
These things will I cherish,
With a glad and thankful heart.

V W Veale

LOSING BATTLE

On the Tunis road in the brazen sun
'midst the mottled wrecks of headlong Hun
I stood and watched the 'Desert Rats'.
As they swung along in their battle hats,
Young brown men - lean of flesh
KD and webbing bleached afresh
And my heart was glad as I watched them go
Singing a song of a German whore
For they'd winded the scent of victory

On a London street in the slanting rain
Thro' November gloom I watched again
Those fewer, sadder greying Rats
As they trudged along in their bowler hats
Withered of muscle and pale of face
Only in bearing they showed a trace
Of the men of all those years before
And my heart was sad as I turned to go
For we all lose the battle with 'Father Time'.

N Allbutt

MY WAR YEARS

I joined the NAFFI
To do my bit -
I really then became a hit.
I mothered the boys
And served them tea
All their problems they brought to me,
I gave them fags
And dinner too
I stayed up late
Well after two,
I did my best to see it through
Did very well
I'm sure that's true,
The war did end
I had to leave
No medals did I ever receive
God bless you boys every one
My memories will linger on.

A Keen

DEDICATED TO THE SEARCHLIGHT CREWS 1939-1945

Beams from searchlights, clustered in the sky
Bombers trapped within
Searchlight crews, are down below
Fighters homing in
Fighter pilot, makes a kill
All through the night, they battle on
With determination and skill
What will the score, be then
Wreckage burning everywhere
Lysanders search the shore
They watched the days, turn into night
And night, turn into day
On outposts that, were wild and bleak
When England stood at bay
Guiding aircraft home to base
Plotting their safe return
When the last all clear was heard
And England's shores were safe
What happened to the searchlight crews
And memories, they could relate.

C Williams

RATIONS

In wartime years, we made things do,
   For most things then we had to queue,
We all kept fowls, in our backyard,
   Cause, our ration of meat, was very hard,
It was nice to have chicken legs,
   And a supply of nice fresh eggs,
Clothing coupons, were like gold-dust,
   Blackout curtains, they were a must,
No lights to show from any bars,
   Hooded headlights on all our cars,
To alter clothes, that was the trend,
   And people called it *Make do, and Mend*,
Petrol was scarce, and hard to get,
   Cycles were popular, but not when wet,
Meat was short, especially ham,
   That's when we had, a tin called *Spam*,
Nylon came out, in place of silk,
   And in the shops came powdered Milk,
Blackout wardens, had to make certain,
   That every house had blackout curtains,
The air-raids came by day, and night,
   But we resisted, with all our might,
The damage, was a sight to see,
   But we just sat, and drank our tea.

Bert Richings

THE AIR RAID SHELTER

My Dad built our air raid shelter,
He said, 'twas good and sound,
The only trouble was, it faced the wrong way round,
It didn't have a door and on concrete sides we'd sit,
There was a stove with a flue, which only once was lit,
For on that cold and starry night, a Fire Warden had to ask
Were we sending smoke signals up, to help the bombers with their
task?
The wind blew in with such a force, that if bombs the house had hit,
We'd all have been finished anyway, choking on smoke and grit.
We had a lot of rain that year, our Dad felt such a fool,
As we told all our neighbours, he'd built an indoor pool.
By time the war was over, we'd stay snug and warm in bed,
For it was clear if the bombs didn't get us, pneumonia would instead.

R Finch

THE UNLUCKY THIRTIETH

They were seven young Flight Sergeants, a most experienced crew,
With twenty nine completed and one more *Op* to do.
The thirtieth was no *Piece of cake*, a trip to the dreaded Ruhr,
But they were all determined to finish their first tour.

Q-Queenie their mighty Stirling had served them well before,
Battling through the barrages and night-fighters by the score,
But on this night their luck ran out, an almost direct hit from *Flak*
Wrecked the starboard outer, still they pressed on - no turning back.

Three Hercules kept snarling, doing the work of four
And icy draughts came swirling through jagged holes punched in the
floor,
But they limped onto the target, dead on track for the bombing run,
Left, left, steady, bombs gone! and their grim work was done.

The Stirling soared, relieved of weight, banked homewards in joyous
flight,
Suddenly, a gunner's shouted warning *Fighter skipper, corkscrew
right.*
The Messerschmitt came hurtling in and raked them on the turn,
By the grace of God no one was hit but the port inner began to burn.

Somehow they staggered back to base, the undercarriage was u/s,
The pilot ordered *Bail out boys, then I'll belly-land this mess.*
He whispered *Come on Queenie we can make it* then *Help us please
dear Lord,*
Not knowing that a five hundred pounder was jammed in the bomb
bay on board.

They picked up his shattered remnants, scattered all over the 'drome
And put the bits into a coffin, no chance of sending them home.
He wasn't awarded a medal, after all, he was only doing his job
And bear in mind he was ruddy well paid with a daily fifteen bob.

In the dusty outback of Australia, his parents knelt to pray
That when the war was over, they might visit his grave one day
In a quiet, green, village churchyard eleven thousand miles away
Where Mother England owed a debt to their only son that she never
                                                    could repay.

John Martin

TIME

If I could turn the clock back one more time
And live again the days of yesteryear
I would see again my friends - so far away
And gently wipe away a falling tear

The days of war would never have been here
My friends would see me here today
A little older - wiser men of peace
Oh! God I wish they had been here to stay

The singing laughing days of my lost youth
The joy and comradeship we knew so well
If I could turn the clock back one more time
And have a different happy tale to tell.

K W Newman

SERGEANT'S MESS

The train was packed - no room at all -
The guard's van was the only place.
Amidst the mail bags soldiers stood -
Amongst them, one who was the *Ace*.

Above their rank, a sergeant he;
Reviewing troops as he passed by;
Below his rank, none dare reply -
Until he came to *me*.

'And what are you?' he asked with scorn.
By this time I had had enough;
I answered to the manner born -
A land girl versus a Sergeant tough.

Our armlets bore a central crown;
(The cup of humility he must sup!)
Pointing to it I said -
'I'm the Major of the Muck-spreaders' -
. . . *That* shut him up!

Ruth Prest

SIR WINSTON CHURCHILL (1874-1965)

High in a realm above this earthly land,
There dwells one greatly held in love and awe
By those who knew or who will ever hear
Of him. Now greater still. Sometimes he sits
In thoughts of days gone by, and then inspired
Paints in effusion from a palette glazed
With Heaven's celestial shades. Then stirs
And contemplates a world divided still,
Which yet pursues its constant search for peace.
A peace which we today might never have.
Yet by the Grace of God, and by the strength
And courage shown by this true man, so led
This land as one in giving of its best.
Whose reassuring voice. Whose very name
Gave life and hope and comfort to the weak.
Turned weakness into strength, and purpose gave
That none might ever seek but victory.
When others of his age had ceased to toil
He served his country in its greatest need
With courage, strength and fortitude of mind,
And yet with patience, tact and brilliance, thus
Shone through the darkest day unfailing light.
Then when the day triumphant dawned, he stood
And heard a grateful nation's voice of praise.
The victory won, he came again in peace
To give once more his service to this land.
Far from the noise of battle now, yet still
Near to the hearts and minds of those he served
With all his earthly might. So sadly missed.
In life a never yielding rock. In death a monument.

John Christopher Cole

OLD AIRFIELD

I lie here still, beside the hill,
Abandoned long to nature's will,
My buildings down, my people gone,
My only sounds, the wild bird's song.

But my mighty birds will rise no more,
No more I hear the engines roar,
And never now my bosom feels,
The pounding of their giant wheels.

From the ageless hill their voices cast,
Thunderous echoes of the past,
And still, in lonely reverie,
Their great dark wings sweep down to me.

Laughter, sorrow, hope and pain;
I shall never know these things again,
Emotions that I came to know,
Of strange young men so long ago.

Who knows as evening shadows meet,
Are they with me still, a phantom fleet;
And do my ghosts still stride, unseen,
Across my face so wide and green?

And in the future, should structures tall,
Bury me beyond recall,
I shall still remember them,
My metal birds and long dead men.

Now weeds grow high; obscure the sky,
O remember me when you pass by,
Listening still, for the distant drone,
Of absent friends returning, home.

W Scott

OH, COME TO THE WAR

Oh, come to war, it's a wonderful war,
With majors and colonels and generals galore,
Not many privates and we need quite a lot,
For some silly reason they get themselves shot.

Oh, come to the war, sign on today,
We will give you a rifle and even some pay.
Transport as well to get you up to the line.
Plenty of ammo, we are sure you'll do fine.

Oh, come to war, it's a wonderful war,
Bring all your friends with you, too.
And if you get shot, we'll supply a white cross,
It's the very least we can do.

So please, oh please come to the war,
For it cannot be fought without you.

D W Owen

RUSSIAN CONVOYS

It's 1942 and I am just a boy going off to sea,
Straight from Naval School to help the Nazi flee,
Fifteen and a half I was with all my life ahead
To see the horrors of Arctic War and all the many dead.
On Russian Convoys so many gave their lives,
To help the poor and needy, so they could survive,
Seeing my shipmates dead is terrible to behold.
I saw a youth bend to help a mate, the sea washed over cold,
And Eternally froze them solid in that stance;
Like statues in ice, in the split second of a glance,
One dreadful day in the freezing blasts,
The U boats came and sunk us very fast
Someone above watched over me, I was quickly snatched,
From those icy seas around us, with speed you couldn't match
Frozen, wet and wounded, from the explosion
My sixteenth birthday in Hospital, I had no notion,
That I had almost lost my legs, the clever Doctor saved.
Or I would be a cripple if my legs I gave,
When fully recovered to sail those seas twice more,
I was lucky not to be torpedoed as I had before.
Years later 1986, a commemorative medal was struck,
Russian Convoy survivors received it, to remind us of our luck
As though we would ever forget the horrors we endured,
And just hope and pray that peace really is secured,
So when you see white berets marching on parade.
Just remember who they are, and all the lives they gave.

B Pim

IN THE AIRMEN'S MESS

After five weeks on a cookery course.
We were let loose on the airmen to do our worst.
There was sack after sack of spuds to be rumbled.
We took out the eyes and nobody grumbled.
So a bit later on, it was a pleasant surprise.
When we had to lay out some Lyon's fruit pies.
I'm sad to say they were the last that we saw.
We were short of most things because of the war.

We took it in turns to go on the bread slice.
It wasn't a smart electric device.
It was turning the handle as fast as can be.
To make enough slices for breakfast and tea.
I picked up one loaf, it really felt light.
On starting to cut it, I got quite a fright.
Two mice were in there having a feed.
I just threw it down very quickly indeed.

At meal times they all poured in with a rush,
Steady now lads, there's no need to push,
The sergeant was there to keep them in order.
If they didn't behave, they'd end up with no dinner.
None of us liked to dish out the meat,
To make it go round, it was quite a feat.
One man grumbled 'Is this the smallest you've got?'
So she gave him a piece smaller!
I bet he felt a *Clot*.

For breakfast on Sundays it was bacon and egg.
That's if they managed to get out of bed.
The one's that did used to sneak round for another.
But we'd serve them again without any bother.
When I had to leave, it was with great regret.
The happy times I had there, I will never forget.

Dorothy Mezaks

A DESERT TALE

The caves at Tura-el-Asmant
Were utilised during the war.
It was No 1 Desert Station,
They housed Workshops and were used for store.
Life couldn't have been *a piece of cake*
For the lads who were stationed there.
And I have often wondered
Whether they found time to stop and stare,
To gaze across the river, to appreciate the view,
To be uplifted by its beauty,
And find peace and enchantment, too.

For . . . while stationed and Tura-el-Asmant
I saw a wondrous sight.
Three Pyramids towered over the sand
Monuments to the Pharaohs' might.
Camels walked and goats grazed on the banks of the Nile
While feluccas sailed idly by.
Fellaheen squatted and laughed 'neath the shady palms.
It was a scene to delight the eye.
And more so in the splendour of a sunrise,
Or a glorious and vivid sunset sky.
When, filled with a deep emotion.
Its sheer beauty made me cry.

Margaret Lygo-Hackett

THE FORTUNES OF WAR

What consequences those words bore!
Neville Chamberlain's *We are at war* . . .
Day of Destiny - the sun did shine
That third of September nineteen thirty nine.
No one could know, could visualise
What six years of war would do to their lives.
Some heard the words they'd come to dread -
A loved one hurt, a loved one dead.
A peacetime pairing by priest's proclamation
That stood not the test of long separation.
For many a soldier or airman or sailor
Read heartbreak words of marriage failure.
While in whirlpool of war others had been
Drawn into liaisons not foreseen.
I thank my God that it proved so to be
That Fate put me in this last category.
From London home torn at seventeen I hated
With fellow employees to Cambridge evacuated.
Yet - through those unlit lanes neath moonlit sky
We walked, talked and knew one another she and I,
And early formed those bonds of the heart
That, through six years of war, though much apart,
Led to lasting marriage and to children born.
True, the years that followed that September morn
Brought much pain to many, but I'm grateful for
The gift to my life from the fortunes of War.

L W Baker

REMEMBER

We have no religion - care nought about that
We scoff at the Padre and all his chat
But things change, when we're told of action next day.
Our thoughts turn to God and we silently pray
Please spare us a Lord - we don't want to die
We've so much to live for - a hesitant sigh
Remember you praying when danger was near
How you prayed to your Maker - driven by fear
Spare a thought for some others - not as lucky as you
Their graves so silent - covered in dew.
You were spared to continue - thank him for this day
Keep in touch always, God's not far away.

Douglas Lakey

AD ASTRA
(THE BATTLE OF BRITAIN)

In a wild flight into the lonely sky
You left the world forever, who can know
What supreme joy you felt where cloud-winds blow
Before you died alone, so far, so high.
You sought the stars through spaces none can fly,
The rushing winds about the sun. Through death
Who could not steal that last intensest breath
You reached the height where those bright stars glide by.
Below, the dark sea swells; below, the land
Lies in black shadows, and the wind and rain
Beat out an endless echo of lost pain;
Beat through the darkness of perpetual night;
But you who won that far off starlit strand
Live now secure amid immortal light.

Diana Momber

THE VETERAN

I saw him just the other day waiting for a bus.
How you keeping? I'm, okay he never made a fuss.
I saw him stop a tiger tank in a field just South of Caen.
And he once kept watch while we all slept in a village near Louver in.
The bus pulled up he climbed aboard the driver couldn't wait.
For God sake get a move on Dad I'm twenty minutes late.
Waterloo and Inkerman The Somme and Elamain.
The despair of their officers the Sergeant Major's pain.
And a man who stopped a tiger tank in a field just outside Caen.
The bus moved off he gave a wave I saw him once again.
Lying by a hedgerow as if it were a game.
He stopped a Royal King Tiger in a field just outside Caen.
So shed a tear for passing years the glory and the fame.
And for a veteran of seventy who stopped a tank at Caen.

Alfred Cook

FALCONARA

Moaning, the wind howls
Wind of the sea,
Groaning, like hosts of ghouls,
Stark reality.

Brazenly the sun beats down,
Burning bush and tree,
Symbols of invasions frown,
Inferno of eternity.

Here are decay and rust,
Fruits of tyranny,
Lost in the ash and dust,
Smiles of the free,

Down from its seat is hurled,
Peace and tranquillity
The flag of battle is unfurled.
Death and uncertainty

Noble arts of noblest strain
Blasted by deviltry,
Will they then for e'er remain
Only a memory.

Or will some power from blood and gore,
Cease with profanity
Create through suffering, toil and war,
A nobler truer humanity.

T O Smith

WESTERN DESERT

Soft arched, the purple desert sky,
Low, the bright stars, shining hung,
Gentle, the warm breeze stirs the air,
God and nature, silent, breathe as one,
Of such a night do poets sweetly dream,
But now the sword outspeaks the broken pen
And I lay restless on the desert sand,
And wait, to kill my fellow men.

Robert Holding

TO ENGLAND

Fair thou art - O would that I
Could see thee in thy Glory
My own dear London's dauntless ruins
That tell a wordless story

Would that some Indian genie kind
My loneliness would pity
And waft me magically away
To England's mightiest city

But no - 'neath azure Eastern skies
Where duty sounds its call
I sit and dream of London - Home
And ponder on it all

This ghoulish, ghastly race to kill
To torture and to rape
That tries to bring great Nations
To the level of the ape

Please God, let Peace come to us soon,
Not for my sake alone,
But for the children, sweethearts, wives.
Who battle on at home

Who wear a cheerful countenance
But in their hearts they pray
O God, please keep him safe and well
And bring him back one day

Can all these prayers unanswered go
Can all these lives be broken
Surely relief will come - and soon.
Was Dunkirk not a token

That *right* would triumph over all
And England under fire
Did not her valiant people prove
That they would never tire

So let it be - I rest assured
That Peace will reign again
That Peace, the British love so much
And battle to obtain

Then from our cities battered hulks
From all the streets so bare
A better England will arise
For all of us to share

An England, fine and clean and strong
(Not choked, as Germans plan)
Where we can walk with pride, and say
Thank God, I'm an Englishman.

P C Glyn

GREEN HILLS FAR AWAY

Lying in my bivvy
When the sun has died at last
And the only sounds
The crunch of distant shells,
I suddenly remember all the days
That were the best,
Far from sand and flies, the reek
Of putrid smells.

Cloudy mist and clammy vapour
Hanging loosely on the hills,
And the fir trees glowing green
Against the sky,
Ice-cold water gurgling, chatt'ring
Down a lonely Highland burn,
And a speckled trout
That's leaping at a fly.

They're the things a Jock
Will turn to
When his inner mind's eye glows,
And the fading night brings near
The fateful hour:
Then he reckons up his chances
Of survival on the morn,
Seeing clearly in his torment
The grim front of battle Lour.

Andrew Todd

THE PRESS SHOP

The first words I heard, as I entered the door
'Er wo fit in, that's for sure
They were spoken by Lil, as she staggered across
To deposit her work on the floor

I couldn't believe, that this was my lot
I'll never survive, was my thought -
It was dismal and dark
But God! Worst of all
The noise had a deafening roar
I'd never been in a Press Shop before!

I started to work, and after a while
I was drilling bomb tubes galore
With the approval of Lil, in no time at all
I was *in* with the workers of war

We all had the same aim
'Twas called, pulling your weight
And we worked day and night, I recall
We'd made up our minds
Whatever the cost
No German would step on our shore.

Ada Lovell

UNTITLED

Why wear the *Burma Star*
Good question my son -
It's to remind me how
Precious a walk is on an English spring day can be,
It's to remind me when I moan about my lot as an OAP,
How precious a glass of cold water can be,
It's to remind me how Malaria can sweat the blood out of me
It's to remind me of lost friends who stopped the march,
Through India to the Middle East, cutting supply routes last war,
It's to remind me I wouldn't now have grandsons to carry on my
family,

It's to remind me I'm bloody lucky
To see a smile of disbelief on your cheeky little face.
It's to remind me I came home,
In spite of everything it's still a much better country
Than it would have been if we had not tried to win and won.

K Edgar

LEAST WE FORGET

Every year November time, with head hung low we stand in line.
This is the time to pause, and think of the dead in all the Wars.
Young men cut down in their prime, for us to have
Peace in our time.
So Politicians try to find, a solution for mankind.
To fight seems so insane,
Was their sacrifice in vain.

L A Taylor

THE ATLANTIC STAR

New Brighton Fair is it still there
I must go back and see
Does the ferry still cross the Mersey wide
It did in 43'

The Liver Birds stood so high
Watched all the ships go by
The girls would stand against the Pier Head rail
To wave the ships goodbye

We sailed out pass the Mersey bar
Away for weeks or more
To guard the straggling convoys
We knew would win the war.

The sea turned from an emerald green
To a lovely muddy brown
We were back in port again
In that friendly northern town.

The year's roll by the memory dims
It all seems like a dream
The things we saw the things we did
Could they have really been

We sit here in our twilight years
Maybe sip a glass of beer
Sometimes we have a little smile
Sometimes a little tear.

Harry C Wragg

TEAMWORK

As I run to my post in the dark
One of a team on the Park
I hope before the next duty tour
The War will be over, then never more
Will I be the one to shout *fire*.
Misfire I hear, my heart drops like a stone
For my sweetheart is one of a team.
I listen as in a dream.
Now some boy must volunteer
To carry the shell away to the clear.
Lord, guide the boy's feet, let him not fall
- Which would bring death to us all -
Will our mind ever forget
The excitement, the danger, and yet
How can the folks back home ever know
The fear, and the lives that we owe
Each to the other. The hope and the trust
Peace will come soon, it surely must.
Five minutes of war our teenage has stolen
Now as mature *adults* we fight on.

The bitter wartime memories fade
As sweeter memories now we've made
Of happy times through fifty years
With but a sprinkling of tears.
We love our daughter and our son,
You see the Teamwork carried on
Since I was Predictor Number One
And he was the man in charge of the gun.

Elsie A Walker

THE CABLE WORKER

Connector ends for aircraft! Cables for ships at sea,
For submarine, and army! That was the job for me
So many wires to sort and put in place
We had no time to slow the pace
On huge drums like cotton reels the cables stood
Row on row tested! Then lagged up and off they would go
Long were the hours we stood! Mind and wires mingling
Thousands of wires passed through our hands
Setting wrist and fingers tingling
Putting them all in order! Repetition day by day
But doing it for our loved ones overseas far away
So intricate! So complicated! So tedious yet we carried on
Then starting on another when that one was done
Before we lagged each cable up we put a note inside
Wishing *some one* victory we were full of national pride
When work was done we went to help the WVS in town
We were young and eager didn't want to let our side down
We knitted socks and comforts for our lads far away
Hoping what little we had done would bring victory one day.

Gladys Mary Kearns

THE SOLDIER

They stood there in their thousands,
     In the cold and falling rain.
They were thinking of the war just done,
     The friends never seen again.

Men cried like babies standing there,
     Not one man felt ashamed.
They thought of the graves in far off lands,
     Of the ones that came back maimed.

At last the procession arrived at the door,
     Westminster was there to atone.
A man whose dead body no one knew,
     The *Unknown Soldier* at last had come home.

A B Hughes

INTAKE DAY

The Sergeant Major is in a state
The New Recruits are very late
He walks towards them smile on face
You know I think you'll like this place
I promise you wont be bored
All your food and free board
Tanks on Brecon Plains on Monday
You will find that quite a fun day
Rifle, range, hands grenade,
Tuesday you can see a lot to choose
Wednesday if your good, will take
A walk just ten miles and you can talk
But first a soldier we must make
Of this I'm sure. It's make or break
You can write home to Mam
Tell her you love chips and spam
Now it comes the time to part
A trained soldier walking tall
To a foreign land go he
Credit to the Sergeant's SWB . . .

M Thorne

THE AMBULANCE TRAIN

In the sidings ready to go not knowing when or where,
Surrounding fields of army trucks were suddenly quite bare.
Then came the news of D Day, at last we are on our way
Down to the coast to meet the boats where the sick and wounded
                                                              lay,
Loaded safely on the train we headed North in haste,
Treatment to give from coach to coach, unload no time to waste.
Back to our base then off again repeating the hospital run
Till orders came for Normandy, our work for now was done.

With cattle trucks and stretchers we worked our makeshift train
Up to the Holland border - load up, then back again
With patients of all nations and German prisoners too.
Meals cooked on the rail-side, while children came to view.

Their straw-coloured hair and sores on cheeks they looked a pitiful
                                                              sight
A whip round for our chocolate bars soon brought cries of delight.
Then off they went soon to return with posies of wild flowers.
For sister, while the boys would sing and entertain for hours.

At last our brand new train arrived we travelled then in style.
Until the war was over we had covered many a mile.

Lorna E Collins

A WOMAN'S LOVE

Two years ago you sailed away
That day I'll ne'er forget
I kept a smile and prayed for strength
Although my eyes were wet
Everything so dear to me
Was in that crowded train
No one knew the stress I felt
Or how my heart did pain
I prayed to God as I do now
To help and guide you dear
And bring you safely back to me
I hope that day is near
When we first meet again my man
I'll know not what to say
But all the love I have for you
My eyes they will convey
To be alone with you my love
And feel your tender kiss
And live again those happy times
We both so sadly miss
But soon the day will come my dear
When I shall gladly be
Facing all life's ups and downs
With you alongside me
So keep that happy smile my love
And remember what I say
Our love will be our shining goal
Roll on reunion day.

G Gant

REMEMBRANCE

A poppy blooms, lest we forget
Remembering we pay our debt
To youthful lives, cruelly cut short
Who gave their all that peace was bought.

Remember what? A soldier's dress?
No glamorous girls we ATS
We didn't have a chance to choose,
High heels? They're hardly marching shoes.

The coldness of our Winter billet?
No; warmness of our friends within it,
And queuing in the rain - what stress!
But comfort of the dining mess.

Crossing the fields on blackest night
Remember still the NAAFI light?
The fun we had; 'twas time to dance.
Forget the war for half a chance.

The hours we worked - so hard and long,
But we would sing a wartime song,
And oh the joy to get a letter!
Spirits were raised, we felt much better.

Remember good? Yes, we must try,
And to the bad times say *goodbye*
Our gratitude must never cease,
For we survived to days of peace.

Joyce Mahoney

THE REFUGEE TRAIN

My mind still wanders yet again
To times we rode the deadly train
India had been split in two
But ere that date much work to do.

One makeshift camp was placed at Wah
The refugees had travelled far
They'd left their homes, belongings too
To make a life which they might rue.

The riots caused horrific pain
Prompting need of a special train
A flat bogey was placed up front
With soldiers armed to take the brunt
Of each attack which always came
As we progressed in hill terrain.

At break of day we filled the train
And crawled away across the plain
Mainly coaches, open trucks too,
Our destination no one knew
At Lalamusa we stopped the night
A station sans water was our plight.

We reached Sadoke at noon next day
When two old ladies passed away
Their graves were dug, with thoughts forlorn,
But then I heard a babe was born.

On the third day Cheharta reached
By now the Indian border breached
Safe from the bullet and the flood
The shrouded form of Freedom's blood.

At Ludhiana my troops detrain
To travel North and start again.

William Austin Pugh

I VESPERI SICILIANI

At night it is
That the full wave of longing
Sweeps over us, like the tide
We never see.

A gentle breeze
Sighs through the dust-white olives
(Far from the Mount - but still
Trees of sorrow).

The starlit sky -
Once a blanket while we slept -
Is bright: brighter than we knew
In our own land.

Nearby vineyards
Throb to the Cicada's song,
Which, cleaving the night's silence,
Intensifies it.

Sometimes a voice
Will hail us from the highway,
Bidding us, in liquid tones,
A pleasant sleep.

All these are new
To us (here at War's behest
But rememb'ring still the joys
Of other days):

And yet they strike
A chord in our memory,
And make us yearn for the sight
Of our own land.

F K Bradley

ALAMEIN

If you have lost so many battles
That defeat has become a way of life,
Remember the battle of El Alamein.
Think of a strip of hard sand,
Part of the vast African desert.
It was there that we halted the advance of darkness,
Causing the light to shine again.
So you, facing your own struggle,
Can turn round the events in your life,
So that the end becomes a beginning,
And all hope returns.

Norman Oakes

UNTITLED

When against Hitler we made a stand
With husband in the Army I worked on the land
The work was hard but we also had fun
And were very tired when the day's work was done
Hoeing, and sowing and toiling in the rain
But it was not entirely in vain
As in my 80th year I am healthy and sound
And can still enjoy working on our own plot of ground.

Joan Rose

ON JOINING THE CONVOY

Deep rooted in my memory there's most certainly one date
That's locked in there forever and of that I have no doubt,
The seventeenth day of January, Nineteen forty three,
The day surmise was ratified, the day we learnt our fate,
The day we filed aboard her, the day that she set out,
The day the Drunken Duchess sailed and carried us to sea.

Chill indeed the morning's breaking, dreary and dark the day,
As with full kit and rifles we scrambled up aboard
Aware with this departure that we'd stepped from England's soil.
With hearts that matched the weather we stowed our kit away
In cramped conditions jostling for the space each strove to hoard
In the hammock-harassed confines there in E deck's grim turmoil.

The murk of the next morning saw us slip our final tether
And the booming of the foghorn moaned our heartfelt valedictions
As we drifted down the Mersey, mist-mantled from the shore.
But by noon Nature repented and blew in brighter weather
And with a glorious gesture pandered to my predilections
Presenting smiling Cumbria. What could I ask for more?

Leaning on the bulwark in nostalgic contemplation
I scanned the panorama for each known familiar place.
Barrow's yards were obvious and Seascale's dunes dull gold,
And the symmetry of Black Combe's cone stood bold in isolation,
But the snow-cloth'd humped horizon gave me no definable trace
Of the Central Fells, the major hills whose memories never grow old.

But, goodbye I said to the summits from Old Man to far Skiddaw
From my catalogue of memories, to each lake, each tarn, each track,
Though merged in that snow skyline in my heart identified.
Though oceans will divide us it is not for evermore
Goodbye Cumbria and England, there's no doubting I'll be back!
Next morning we took station in the convoy on the Clyde.

S J Randle

ON LOOKING BACK

I remember that thirteenth birthday of mine, way back in April 1939.
'You're almost grown up now, the first of your teens, and do you
know just what it all means?' said dad. The big wide world is
ahead of you with places to see and things to do, so make each day
count, yes everyone and work hard for your living but make time
for fun. Learn all you can so that you'll know the score'
Fat chance, by September we were at war, and schooldays were
over
soon after that when enemy bombs laid our schools flat.
Days filled with fear and terror at night, bombings, fires, blackouts
with no end in sight. Losing our loved ones at Dunkirk or at sea.
Not quite what a teenager's life ought to be.

But on my seventeenth birthday I did what I'd planned, I joined the
Royal
Air Force to help fight for my land and I never regretted the choice
that I'd made, though the harshness of war made me sad and afraid.
The good friends I made and the many I lost, all added up to a
terrible cost, but I learned how to handle the sorrows and joys
and my colleagues who died in my thoughts are still boys.
It just wasn't worth it all the hurts and the pain, the world makes
those mistakes again and again, we seem to learn nothing, do we
even try, perhaps we were just born to kill and to die.

But then it was over, there was peace in this land, all flattened
and derelict, where we'd made our stand.
We will rebuild it, yes we'll have a go, to make a land fit for
heroes where our children can grow, to be healthy and happy,
educated and free, yes all of those things we never could be.
So we worked and we planned this would be our fate, to make Britain
a nation that once more was great.
Now we are weary and our struggles cease. We won the war but lost
out in the peace.

And I'm an old lady, you know, an OAP and the nation suggests
I'm a liability. A bed blocker, a fool, a parasite, a leech, and
that's only quoting the media's speech.
The object of this is to make it quite clear, if we hadn't had the
bottle, you wouldn't be here.

M Couchman

THE INSPECTORATE

Working twelve hours each and every day,
Gave little time for rest and play,
Anxious our armaments order to complete,
To supply our desperate naval fleet,

Both men and women made bombs and shells,
While we made sure they were made darn well,
Watching each process from beginning to end,
For accuracy our sailors rely and depend,

Two pounders; SAP's to a 4.5" shell,
Hedgehogs, depth charges, torpedoes as well,
Danger involved hardly crossed our minds,
More danger walking through a field of mines,

All rules and safety precautions we had to adhere,
Avoid complacency then there is nothing to fear,
Only the enemy who threatened us many times,
Once following our train along the lines,

A puff of smoke gave the game away,
But somehow we managed to lead him astray,
Thousands travelled each day by bus and train,
In sunshine, ice, blizzards and pouring rain,

Without warning a lone raider one moonlight night,
Was heading homewards when we came into *his* sight,
He swooped, guns blazing spraying us with flak,
No-one was hurt but we know *he* didn't get back,

A daylight raider dropped a bomb one day,
But missed, so preventing a mighty firework display,
Most days and nights the eerie sirens blared,
When we all huddled in the shelters scared.

Hilda B Burchell

SET FAIR FOR FRANCE

As we pulled from the shore, I thought of home
Would I ever see it again?
I stood with my thoughts, sea breeze on my face
Surrounded by quiet men
Slowly the shore disappeared from view
From side to side we tossed
Our eyes now searching for Normandy
Each man with his thoughts engrossed

Too soon we reached the coast of France
Through the water onto the beach
The rolling sound of thundering guns
A sound we would very soon reach
This wasn't training, this was for real
So nerves now came into play
It is a feeling I'll never forget
I remember it to this day.

There were many testing times to come
Oft times you would hold your breath
A putrid smell pervaded the air
The sickening odour of death
And when our Padre was killed, it shook me
Didn't God look after his own?
But someone up there must have liked me
For I returned safely back home.

J Newman

I WAS THERE

I was there at Gettysburg, as I was at Waterloo,
Where I did the kind of work that only I can do.
I saw the young survivors take time out from the fight,
To lay their fallen comrades down their faces drawn and white.

I was there along the Somme, at Passchendaele, Verdun,
Where I did my patient work until that work was done.
I heard the measured footsteps of the slow march for the dead
The skirl of pipes, the muffled drums, the volleys overhead.

And I was at El Alamein, Salerno, Normandy,
At Singapore, in Burma, many lands across the sea.
There was no time for weeping nor for any childish fears,
The sorrows and regrets would come in all the after years.

The morning sun has dawned anew but never more with these,
The hearts of those who went from here were not again at ease.
For them there was no splendour in the victories they had won,
They knew the cost and mourned each dreadful day
It had been done.

Yet they will always need me, for war is not a game,
They'll need me most when e'er a generation has slain.
And I'll be here forever, with no claim to rank or class,
For I am nothing more than just the cool and silent grass.

W R Halliday

TO THE GALLANT FOURTEENTH ARMY

They loved their Scottish homeland,
Their scented English lanes,
They loved their great Welsh mountains
The gentle Irish rains,
But now they sleep in Burma
Where the Chindwin River flows,
A small white cross above their heads,
Their names? Their comrades know.

They view their little village streets,
When the lights did gleam like pearls,
They liked their pictures and their dance,
Their pretty village girls,
Their youth was one brief glory,
Which sped too quickly by,
They left this happy homeland,
And crossed the sea to die.

Unfurl the flag of freedom,
Salute your glorious Sons,
They came from every walk of life,
To man, and fire the guns,
And through the skies across the seas,
O'er many foreign lands,
To match their British courage,
Against the heathen bands.

Yes! When all this is over,
And peace once more returns,
We'll think of those we left behind,
As we watch the homefires burn,
We'll think of all those gallant lads,
Neath Burma's sweating soil,
Who made the supreme sacrifice,
The Japanese to foil.

From Dimapur to Kohima,
Through Imphal's bloody plains,
This battle raged for many months,
In heat and monsoon rains,
Through Burma's steaming jungles,
Along the Tiddim road,
Then up the chocolate staircase,
Their gallant way they strode.

The road across the frontier,
Lead into Mandalay,
And there folks left for Tokyo,
We know no other way,
When the rising sun has set for good,
And freedom flag will fly,
Salute the Fourteenth Army,
They weren't afraid to die.

Sleep on you unsounded heroes,
You died! But not in vain
You will always be remembered,
Fourteenth Army is your name.

William Lewis

TROOPING 1940

Leaving Gourock with the tide,
  Slipping slowly down the Clyde.
One thought then doth fill your brain,
  Will I e'er come home again.

They showed us our boat stations,
  But there were not many boats.
They've told us not to worry,
  There are plenty of Carley Floats.

We lay at anchor in Freetown's bay,
  Sweating all night, baking all day.
Then on until in two days time,
  We celebrated *Crossing of the Line*.

Bored stiff, feeling lousy,
  Solo, Brag, Housey Housey.
Every mess deck had its banker,
  Poker, Pontoon, Crown and Anchor.

Natal was like a bit of heaven,
  Mombassa was pleasant as well.
Aden just like an open oven,
  But Massawa was surely like hell.

We watched the Dolphins play for hours,
  Queued up for sea water showers.
Caught Gyppy Tummy, always runny,
  Stinking Heads, not so funny.

Welcomed at Tewfik by dirt, and flies,
  And the Khamseen blowing sand in eyes.
But *Maleesh* there was blancoing to do
  For on the morrow we went up the Blue.

S G Dollimore

PRIVATE ATKINS - AND SON

We were in the thickest part of it
When the bugles said, *Cease fire*;
We couldn't understand it quite
As we wallowed in the mire.
But the Jerries came towards us, sir,
And we went to meet them too;
'It's over now,' we shouted, sir,
'So now what do we do?'

We came home to dear old England, sir,
And they cheered us, waved us flags;
They toasted us and speechified,
And gave us feeds and fags.
And then they all forgot us, sir,
Except the wife and kid
Who day by day got thinner, sir,
On dole just o'er a quid.

Our country didn't want us then,
Or so we used to complain,
Until the Germans rose once more
And war broke out again.
There were just three things that held me back -
One arm, one leg, one eye,
But Sonny's gone to take my place -
He'll win all right - or die.

Dunkirk, Benghazi and Tobruk,
El Alemein and Crete -
He's seen the world much more than we,
In victory and retreat.
I suppose the day will soon be here
That he'll come marching past,
And none will cheer him more than me
When war is won at last.

But cheering him and toasting him
Won't give my lad much start
Unless we really mean it, sir,
And keep the peace at heart.
If Sonny's got to join the ranks
And file in for his dole,
Like *I* did when we won *our* war -
His need will damn my soul!

John Nichols

H-HOUR D-DAY

In the throat a twiggy harshness,
Breathes a rasping ragged thrush,
The heart's clutch juddering its fear
Please! Isn't H hour almost here.

A muffled curse, stubbed toe, chink of metal,
Night fast losing its cloying thickness
To thin drear streaks of greying mist.
It's on, we're off, whose first - not me.

Rope netting harsh on sweating palms
Rusty paint tears a nail, scrapes a knuckle
What fool can waste breath to chuckle
You who would be first, now hold back.

The last six feet, a drop to a jarring slam
Why does sweat cascade behind an ear
Thick tongue swallowing the bile of fear
Needless, since it can't surmount the craven throat.

Move off; the landing craft scrambling sound
Mercifully drowns the whir of approaching metal
Hail, of probing death, that's all around
Whispering to whimpering mouth with fear held close.

Spray breaks over freeboard - a near miss,
A sudden yaw, looks up, coxswains arm hangs loose
Another hauls on spokes to right her
A crescendo of noise heralds the near objective.

A grating heave grinding on an underwater obstruction
Slowing, spilling off to starboard, rights, then on
Rattle of chains, then the ramp's downward
Thump, wading knee deep through reddened spume.

Leaden legs heave against the shingle
A tugging plucks at webbing pack makes
A stumble left involuntary movement beneath
A foot, a searing jerk and crack.

Thoughts like disturbed minnows dart about
It's over, I can stay here safe, be thankful
Soon to return to safety and sanity, and yet
Is this what it was all for; a broken ankle?

George Kay

INTO BATTLE

How sore and tired were their feet,
Those men marching to the beat,
Sergeant shouting Left and Right,
As on they marched in the Dawn light,
Sound of Gunfire in the distant ahead,
Many wishing they were home in bed,
Backs bent with their heavy load,
How tired they were and it showed,
Suddenly the steady beat of a drum,
From the front of the column did come,
Then the strains of the Pipes played,
It seemed those men were saved,
The straightening of every man's pack,
As they eased their heavy pack,
A spring came in their heavy tread,
As the Pipers in front strongly led,
No more need for the Sergeant's Left, Right,
Those men could march now all right,
Into the battle those men went,
To save their country so hell bent,
How many were left
We do not know,
But what brave men
What a show.

J S Johns

SACRIFICE

I've never been a man of letters;
Few brains I have seem locked in fetters.
My old lass . . . I call her *Katy*,
Like me, her years, well past eighty;
Says *I clean and cook and you I nurse,*
Let's see if you can enter a verse.
Reaching for my baccy. My pipe I light;
Dear *Katy* thinks I am awfully bright.
'Remember back . . . still only a lad;
Village folk thought you were mad.
For King and Country . . . sixteen, a rookie raw
You went off to fight ole Hitler's war.
There were no retreats . . . just advance,
Step by step . . . across stricken *France*.
Through mud and on through puddles of gore,
Jack my lad . . . always to the fore.
Wounded . . . agonised with pain;
Not one word did you complain.
The General said, in his entire career
He'd never met such a man without fear.
He saluted. Cheers rang out from the rest
As he pinned the VC to your chest.
'Surely Jack . . . you must concede
A great story if you will tell of your deed.'

What I'd tell . . . if it would help mankind,
War rewarded me . . .
One arm
And I'm blind.

Tom E Chilton

BURMA ADMIN BOX 1944

Through jungles thick, we made our way
Would we make it through the day
And the steaming forest heat
With aching limbs, and stinking feet
The leeches cling, mosquitoes bite
I wonder if we'll make the fight.
Then the nips crawled up behind
No way out then could we find.
They had us caught, the yellow fox.
So then we formed the admin box.
They pinned us down for many weeks.
No water in the dried up creeks.
No more food left in the larder.
Life was getting so much harder
No good news to cheer the day
The postman never came . . . this way
Our bodies housing clingling crabs.
Prikley heat and ringworm too leaving nasty little scabs.
How long since we got supplies
God how I'd love to close my eyes.
Flies dived in; and out of watery stew.
No tea left, to make a brew.
But came the day, when all was well.
We fought and fled that stinking hell
Lots we left, so cold and dead
To sleep deep in their earthly bed.

E K Wood

UNTITLED

I was a conscript in the Army in *World War Two*
It was an experience through and through.
The world was in a shocking mess
Full of much gloom and sadness.
My travels took me to France, Germany and India
Some of which were lands of wonder
I went on ships and returned by air
And I did some things I should never dare.
My Army stories would fill a book,
Although the time was short it took.
I was taught how to drive a tank
And I got promoted to NCO rank.
Friends were made and many were lost,
The war was fought at a dreadful cost.
When it was over we could afford a smile.
In retrospect it was all worthwhile.
The tyrants that caused it were all soon caught.
Three cheers for those who stood and fought.

Dennis R Boswell

THE ANZIO BEACHHEAD
(ITALY 1944)

Where are they now!
  Those gallant men who fought at Anzio,
And with whom I was proud to serve alongside,
  Those hard won battles, to hold the beachhead.
That small piece of Italy, so quickly taken,
  That the enemy was shaken.
It was a *combined operation*,
  By men from the United Kingdom and the USA
The landings, took the enemy by surprise,
  And they were under no illusions,
That Rome, was the prize.
  We failed to exploit our advantage,
And the enemy, was quick to reverse the situation.
  So unable to move, forward or back,
We consolidated and held on,
  Despite many a determined counter attack.
Because the enemy held all the high ground,
  His guns, at any target could pound;
And everything and everybody was observed.
  Because of stacked ammunition, along the roads,
There were notices stating *dust brings shells*.
  We had to move at night, and we got many a fright.
Make any sound, and they sent over a mortar round.
  But our twenty five pounders, broke up many an attack.
We head out, and after a four months bout,
  And a terrific barrage, we finally broke out.
Rome fell to the Allies on the Fifth of June
  With regimental bands, playing a lively tune.
We then came out of the *line*
  And were sent back to rest in Palestine.

Tom Leech

BELGIUM (CHRISTMAS 1944)

He was a priest;
  And for a moment's time
We stood - then walked across
  The devastated place.
He clasped his hands together
  In despair.
Looked at the dead,
  And the bewildered dying.
And in God's Holy name
  Blessed them.
And those that could, answered
  When he said, *What is your name*?
And some lived long enough
  To say *Amen*.
When he, the priest
  Absolved them from their sins.
I walked away and lit a cigarette,
  Looked at the sky
Saw clouds serene and free.
  Watched this priest
To whom names meant so much;
  As if he was an auditor for God
Making a tally for the eternal book.
  Nearby a bitch in whelp,
Too tired to flee this busy place of death.
  Whimpered in pain.
I knelt beside her
  Fondled her weary head.
'What is your name?' I said
  And held her close to me
And wept.

D C Denton

ZERO '42

Cold
In the short days of February
The cold is numbing;
Snow and packed ice everywhere -
Grateful for my khaki greatcoat.
Cold
Square-bashing, route marches.
Cold
In the tepid shower, shivering, get dressed quickly.
Hurry up, outside, Squad 14.
Unfamiliar clothing clings to half-dry skin.
Cold
In bed, the coal-fired stove remote.
Cold
On nightshift, fingers numb on radio controls.

The respite of summer passes.

Cold
Hospital in winter is no joke,
Bleak open-fronted ward in zero temperature.
The cage beneath my blankets allows the penetrating chill
To circulate around my limbs.
I try to stretch my injured leg,
Cold steel splint restricting movement.
Cold
I could not be much colder if I were dead.
How long, I wonder
Will this cold war go on?

Margaret Leckie

DOING MY BIT

It seems like it was yesterday
As I sit and dream of the past . . .
When life for me changed completely
The years have sped so fast.

The day was sunny, June, forty one
I'd never travelled alone before . . .
Would I find the camp before midnight?
I did . . . with so many more.

Life became hectic, rules to obey
No civvies now, just Army gear . . .
PT at dawn, parade ground drill
Yet we grew to enjoy it, 'twas clear.

Training completed, new postings
Where we settled to Army life . . .
Dodging those bombs, daytime and night
But our youth helped us cope with the strife.

Postings were frequent, but often sad
Leaving friends caused us much pain . . .
For we knew quite well as we said goodbye
We never would meet again.

When the war was finally over
And I was a civvie once more . . .
I emerged a confident person
Not the shy naive girl as before.

There were times that were both sad and happy
But few that caused us real pain . . .
I found it a wonderful experience
And looking back . . . I would do it again.

Catherine A Fincher

WE ALL PLAYED OUR PART

During the long years of World War Two
Everyone did the best that they could do
Young men and old joined the Home Guard to fight
If Hitler should invade our shores day or night
Women did the jobs that men used to do
In factories, shipyards and on the land too
As postwomen and bus clippies they did their part
Many joined the forces from the start
Young men volunteered to join in the fray
In the forces they fought till victory day
As children we too helped in the war
By collecting the salvage by galore
Later I camouflaged nets to disguise
The tanks and guns from the enemies eyes
Mothers they eked out the rations each day
While dads grew veg to keep the wolves at bay
Older men too joined the ARP
They helped when the raids were as bad as can be
So truly we all played our part don't you see
To help keep Britain The Lands of the Free.

Marguerite Layton

THE FEW

Out of the blue they came, young
men proud in all their untried
youth, snapping their fingers in
the face of death, defying the
uneven odds.

The laughing boys, scrambling to
the fight no thought of sorrow
they rode the tops of clouds, close
to the breath of God, careless of
their unused tomorrows.

Flying into the sun, a few against
the many saving all our future days
by giving theirs, believing in right
and truth they gave us their bright
and lovely days, and all the dreams of
Youth.

Catherine Neale

A NIGHT IN THE OPS ROOM - A PLOTTER'S TALE

It's *All Quiet* on the Board - not a plot in sight,
Ops Room Crew is praying for a trouble free night.
Filter Room checks that Station Plotters are still on the line,
And Observer Corps contacts saying. *Everything's fine.*
The Controller is puzzled by the lack of flurry.
He appears somewhat restless and shows signs of worry.
He says he's got *a gut feeling* and makes pretty clear
To those on the *Dais* his suspicions and fear.
An air of eerie expectancy hovers around
But apart from the *Filter* checks there's hardly a sound.
It's all very strange for there's *A Bomber's Moon*
And a deep disquiet pervades the room.
It's *All Quiet* on the board - not a plot in sight.

The handset furiously rings and shatters the calm,
It's the Observer Post calling to raise the alarm.
The message that's given brings shock and dismay.
'There's hundreds of bombers coming this way!'
'Action Stations - Action Stations,' the whole camp is alerted,
NAAFI, Messes and Billets are quickly deserted.
Group, surprised, tells the Plotters *Stand by for Block Raid*
Swiftly a tin-hatted WAAF has red arrows displayed.
The Station's two Fighter Squadrons cannot get off the ground.
A bomb drops, buildings shudder, fear and menace abound.
Upwards and onwards planes and plots wend their way,
Map activity ceases . . . They're out of group and away.
Panic over for now . . . There's not a plot in sight.
People anxiously wonder *who's been pasted tonight!*
A phone rings, then *Ops B*, who seems in a daze,
Says . . .
'Coventry's *had it* . . . the whole City's ablaze!'

Margaret Lygo-Hackett

A CALL TO ARMS
SUNDAY 3RD SEPTEMBER 1939

Give up your chores, the bugle sounds;
Till quieter times all else must wait;
A greater challenge now abounds -
The grim aggressor at our gate.

Just as your fathers did before,
Take up your arms the foe to face;
Committed to this second war
So soon to test our island race.

Keep open wide the seven seas,
That all our lifelines stay intact,
And show that by securing these
Britannia Rules The Waves is fact.

Stand firm to guard our sceptred isle;
On high alert each tank and gun.
Prepare for that awaited trial -
In France to meet the dreadful Hun.

Let every plane patrol our skies;
Let no marauder through at will;
Be ever searching with keen eyes,
And ever lurking for the kill.

Whatever may the future hold;
However long and hard our plight;
Let now the enemy be told
That Britain's ready for the fight.

James R B Hinton

THE BOAT

The Blighty erk his weary way has trod
   Each day to *A* Flight on *DI* and *mod*;
A fearful ogre stalks this wretched bod
   And seeks to pluck him from his native sod - The Boat!

Away from Mum and Dad and sisters too,
   Away from his dear sweetheart fond and true,
Away from all the things he likes to do;
   'Twill even stop his drinking NAAFI *brew* - The Boat.

And now the dreaded day is drawing near
   The airman is consumed with mortal fear,
Tries drowning sorrows in good English beer:
   Next morning - there it is - beside the pier - The Boat.

O'er next three years now let us draw the veil,
   The bod's complexion is no longer pale,
His only joy is far-from-frequent mail
   And thoughts of that which hits the homeward trail - The Boat.

Words like *Kiswaste, Kitna baje hai,*
   He utters now and bats not lid of eye,
He even speaks to *bibbis* on the sly
   But only one thing interests the guy - The Boat.

At last a notice meets his questing gaze,
   It warns all *39s* to count the days:
That's been *his* group from far-off Bevin days;
   Now soon upon her ample decks he'll laze - The Boat.

O blessed, beauteous belle of all the brine,
   Your fifteen knots is writ in every line,
Though Blighty weather may be wet or fine
   Return him to his home beside the Tyne - O Boat!

Reg Dyer

A CASTLE IN WARTIME

The story of a Castle,
A wartime tale,
Memories of *World* War Two,
And of the beautiful Vale.

Fascination for me,
A very young Lass.
A Clippy, on a Bus,
Run by Gas.

The sight of the *Doughboys*,
Trooping out of that Castle,
Bustling, noisy,
Causing no hastle.

On the evening bus service,
They would clamour for a ride,
Uniforms immaculate,
Worn with Pride.

With a *ding* on my Machine,
Their fares I'd collect,
And as I called out *Fares please*,
Paid with respect.

A Bus full to capacity,
Of American Guys,
Fond memories for me,
Of those cheerful GIs.

For these *Yanks,* with their Jeeps,
It was the Law,
Soon they moved on,
To fight the War.

Grace Burnett

DIEPPE

Many a man gave his life today,
British, Canadian, American too,
They went through Hell their parts to play,
In doing their duty for you.

Their chances were oh! So very slight,
They were outnumbered by many to one,
But they did not hesitate to fight;
For each Hun's ounce they gave a ton.

They blazed away as a sample
Of what mettle our men are made
And, when they landed, it was not they,
But the Hun who was most afraid.

What stirring adventures, courageous
They made, as they powered their way thro',
Their spirit and action spontaneous,
Their shots each aimed well and true.

Let us give thanks to our Air Force too,
And our Navy who did their job well,
For helping their comrades in action,
And bringing some back from Hell.

This day I shall always remember
In memory of those men tho' few,
Who, in giving their lives, did render
Their greatest service to you.

So the mothers, the wives and sweethearts
Of these bravest and manliest of men,
They fought that you and all people
May live in peace again.

T E Davies

THE EMPIRE'S NAVY

There are stories you've heard of our Navy's fame
As they take every part, like playing a game
There's nothing so grand as to see those boys fight
To bring down old Jerry in the midst of a fight
Now the raid is over and they stand to rest
Waiting for Jerry to bring out his best
The Cruisers, Destroyers and others, they stand
To see that the troops are safely on land
Not only the Gunners are in this fight
Just think of the Stoker in the rotten plight
While down below on his dirty job
Working, sweating and praying to God
To save his ship, his mates and his life
While most of the time he thinks of his wife
Then there are Bunting and Motor Mechs too
Who have, in their part, their bit to do
Now you can search any country from east to west
Who can beat our sailors when at their best
The Navy, as you know, has never lost
Because they know what would be the cost
They fight for their country, families and Crown
So don't ever worry they won't let you down
Now I've come to the end of my short story
And in it I mean the Empire's Glory.

W J Horsley

UNTITLED

From eighteen until twenty-four,
I waged my stint in the six year war.
I worked till I could hardly stand,
In doing my bit, slaving on the land
Which was growing food to feed us.

Our pay was small, our beds had dents
Beneath those clumsy canvas tents,
But all the time our thoughts were turned,
To family and friends for whom we yearned
And who were *over there*.

About the end of forty-three,
When a machine gun fiend tried to end it for me
I decided, when talking to elders and betters
To take on the job of delivering letters
To folks who were aching for news.

Through winter, summer and winter again
I took their letters, in wind, sun, and rain
Delighted when their happy smiles
Confirmed what I thought, that across the miles
A message had come from a loved one

Sadly, that job then came to an end
When on a visit to a friend
A V2 fell and spread its load,
Right on a factory along her road
And I lost an eye.

Isobel E Crumley

THE UNKNOWN WARRIOR

They joined the local Army Force,
Territorials they were called at the time.
Attached to the Beds and Herts, of course.
All young lads, nearly in their prime.

Alas came the sound of distant guns.
For them, a job has to be done.
Off they went, friends and Mother's Sons.
To the Far East, their jobs begun.

Most of them died in tragic ways.
Or disappeared, one knows not where,
Others in Hell Camps spend their days.
Survivors experiences they wouldn't share,

Years later, wandering after the war,
This clearing in the jungle was found,
North of the place known as Singapore.
Among plants overgrown, an unkempt mound.

Amid tall grasses, a feeling of dread,
An exposed mound, six foot by two foot six.
Old rifle, with a helmet, rusty red.
Headstone for some lad, feelings are mixed.

He could have been one of our lads,
So many missing, never to return.
Many more out there makes life so sad.
Tears by Family and Friends, their faces burn.

Remember, lonely mound, helmet rusty red.
Name not known, or how he died I fear.
No headstone, or eternal flame by his head.
The Unknown Warrior from Bedfordshire . . .

C Robertson

SPITFIRE JOHNNY

The dishevelled man walked through the town,
He always had a mirror in his hand.
To see his antics made people frown,
No one knew, how could they understand.

He lived day by day in his tortured life,
Wandering with his mirror, his trusted friend.
Nothing mattered, no Family no Wife.
Only himself to worry about until the end.

When he was young and in Airforce Blue.
He eventually patrolled the dangerous sky,
Till one day, he forgot what he should do.
Look in your mirror, forgot? Why oh! Why?

He felt the heat from the enemy shells,
As they exploded in an awful flash.
He felt the nausea, pain and the sound of bells.
But he floated down, whilst his plane crashed.

In hospital his wounds were on the mend.
Alas his mind couldn't take the strain,
Cruel people thought he was round the bend,
Thinking of the mirror had scrambled his brain.

Years went by, he was in a terrible state.
His small crazy world stayed day by day.
Mirrors reminded him, Look out, alas too late.
The tortured mind was the price he had to pay.

The day came when he was laid to rest.
Mirror in hand, face at last in peace.
His roaming done, medals on his chest.
Spitfire Johnny, it's a happy release.

C F Armstrong

POPPIES FOR REMEMBRANCE

See the petals falling, in remembrance of the dead,
See the petals falling, red, red, red:
Not flowers, just single petals, each one
shaken from the stem of life;
for their early death was a sacrifice
of War and bloody strife.

See the petals falling, so we never, never forget,
See the petals falling, red, red, red:
Each one represents a sorrow, for those
whose loved ones never came home,
and here we share their sad remembering
aware nothing can atone.

See the petals falling, falling, lest we forget,
See the petals falling, red,
                    red,
                        red!

Mary S Evans

REMEMBERED STILL (ON A VISIT TO NORMANDY)

Lush green fields and sandy beaches,
Along the coast of Normandy;
They set the scene for memories
Flooding back to reality.

We stood once more on foreign soil,
Lowered standard gently blowing;
A motley throng be-medalled there
So reverently remembering.

The trimmed green grass; a white stone cross;
Many headstones all neatly rowed;
The quietude that filled the air;
The reverence of heads all bowed.

Mental finger gently stirring,
Seeking deeply within the mind;
Searching the depths for memories
And names of those we left behind.

Places, happ'nings, from former days;
The sadness there, that still prevails;
Pegasus bridge; Arromanches;
The Beach; The Dunes; Church Spires; Coursuelles:

Sea caressing the casualties;
Flotsam of War; a wood; a hill;
But most of all, faces are seen
That grow not old, remembered still.

H Val Horsfall

DUTY

There are things in life you must hide
But now I must take you to one side
To tell you of the life I led
The reason why I shot him dead
In a camp across the sea
Serving the King for my Country
Our biggest enemy was not the sand
But natives in this foreign land
While on guard one moonlight night
Three men approached, and what a sight
They staggered forward all forlorn
All as naked as they were born
Sometime later I patrolled the tents
I remembered all too well this incident
The natives robbed the tents with success
We were humiliated with some distress
I saw him going through the trees
I ran, a trip wire brought me to my knees
He moved, not to the road, but towards the sea
Kicking out, sten gun in hand, I was free
Dragging kit bags made him slow
With sten gun to hip I let go
He dropped somewhere in the sand
As I nursed my injured hand
That native worked at the camp store
Wouldn't rob us anymore
I'm sorry it happened that way
And yes, I regret it to this day.

William R Dean

86

DISTANT DAYS AND DOLPHINS

Standing right for-ard in the bows,
Stripped to the waist beneath a blazing sun,
Blown spume from waves drying before it had begun to feel wet,
He watched the dolphins play,
None but they could say, the simple pleasure that they found,
Of rolling round to dart in and out of the bow wave,
Beneath a blazing blue pacific sky,
They radiated the joy of life,
Perhaps that was why he felt a need of them,
Standing there alone,
He could recall the seven days leave he never had,
Solitary up in the bows he felt unutterably sad,
His only balm the dolphins,
Remembering how he and his wife of one day,
Fingers entwined, walked happily into his home,
To be faced with a telegram recalling him by first train,
Putting into two lives aged eighteen and nineteen a pain,
That was to last two years,
Or that he would see in cloudless blue skies,
The light blue of her eyes,
Or skittering rays of sunlight,
Bouncing golden off the waves before they fled,
Would remind him of a golden head so many miles away,
Love and loving were so much like the sea he thought,
Plumbing unknown depths, holding unknown storms,
And answering to the ebb and flow of life,
With havens in which lay the untold peace of loving hearts,
Thoughts of the mind, which he could only find,
The dolphins to share them with.

R H Higgins

FALAISE

Sun in August, long hot days.
Warmth and comfort, summer haze.
Scent of flowers.
Happy hours.

Sights and sounds of a country fair.
Festive spirit, joyful air.
Laughing children, divorced from care.

Balloons, ice-cream, bunting, sweets.
Festooned hedges, coconut treats.

Peaceful, tranquil, those summer days.
Sad-spoiled now, recall Falaise.
Remembered ever, horror stays.
Country afire, raging blaze.

The enemy trapped, noose near tight.
Struggle to flee, continue to fight.

Horror, filth, stink, disease.
Thick like mist, unmoved by breeze.
Mouth closed tight, gasp not for breath.
Dead men, horses, black, belch death.

Smell of hell on summer days.
Blood and screams, vile carnage.
Dwell forever in that place Falaise.

Sons of mothers, twisted, broken.
Arms and legs, strewn battle token.
Typhoons, guns, rocket, shell.
Created monstrous, stench-filled hell.

Entrails of man, and lowly beast.
Festooned hedges, macabre, a feast.
For fat-bellied flies,
Too heavy to rise.

The days of the fair on warm summer days.
In that place of death, that place Falaise.

Graham Lewis

THE LONELY WATCHER

Huddled for warmth on an open bridge
four bells struck the hour before dawn
eyes tired and sore from the bitter cold winds
keeping watch on this December morn

At daylight's first break would an enemy strike
each lookout then fully aware
if a sighting was missed and a torpedo hit
his ship would need more than just prayer

The minutes dragged on, close your eyes, look again
was a periscope there to be seen
with fear as the spur keeping tired men awake
seeking light where the darkness had been

Without warning the peril each lookout had feared
a moment of terror then came
the torpedo struck with a horrific crash
chaos in towering flame

The smoke drifted on revealing Her scars
no chance of survival, indeed
with almost a third of the ship having gone
they must take to the boats with all speed

Below decks the reaper had taken His toll
many young lives had been claimed
The U-boat had fled lest vengeance appear
in warfare they could not be blamed

On the platform above port side of the bridge
a lookout stared down at the sea
the watch he thought lonely now lonelier still
why take my shipmates, not me?

John E Barnard

TO THOSE WHO DIED

The bleak spring of peace
Breaks o'er a war-worn world
Giving life a further lease
To those whose banners were unfurled
Pledged to their desperate cause
Of wresting freedom from Satan's claws.

Weary were those who waited
Grim and tired were those who fought
And those there were who were fated
To die for the cause they sought.
Through giving all, they gave
A new path of peace to pave.

They will not see summer follow
Spring, after the winter of strife,
Nor will they ever know
Again, the gloriousness of life
And we, who are left, will sigh
For we, saw them die.

Norman Acaster

A GREAT OCCASION - D DAY

We had boarded our craft the previous day,
But the weather turned rough so HQ said to stay,
We lay offshore in the bay overnight,
Each man with his memories locked in tight,
Thinking back to those happy June days,
When we lived our own lives and went our own ways,
To the country maybe or down to the shore,
Day after day we would go back for more,
Take a trip on the ferry, almost four miles,
Hundreds of faces all full of smiles.
Lots of ice-cream, lemonade and cakes,
No wonder some days we had tummyaches.
Most thinking of loved-ones somewhere or other,
My thoughts drifted back to my dear mother,
I pictured the anguish she had in her eyes,
On my last leave when we said our good-byes,
She had guessed what was coming but hadn't let on,
There'd be tears in her eyes long after I'd gone.
I suddenly realised our craft had moved,
How well we were trained was soon to be proved.
Those years of training had come to a head,
By the end of the day there would be many dead.
The Armada sailed on over the swell,
Soon we were entering the jaws of hell,
Bombs, shells, the mortars there were galore,
Everything hit us as we neared the shore,
Worse days we'd see 'til peace we would find,
But that first day will live in my mind,
For the day we set out on the great invasion,
Was also the date of an important occasion,
'Twas the 6th of June we went over the sea,
It was also my 21st birthday you see.

James Nelson

RUDE AWAKENING

'Dear God' I thought 'Is that *my* face?'
That glass will have to go
I knew one day that I'd grow old
But this is quite a blow.

The sagging jaw, the wrinkled face
The hair now turning white.
It's just as well the failing eyes
Don't clearly see the sight.

The aches and pains 'That's part of age'
or so the doctors say
'Just take these pills, the red ones first
Then blue ones twice a day.'

No longer can I walk the hills
Or brave the wintry showers,
Since that last cold can't taste a thing
Nor even smell the flowers

In darker moments - in the *slough*
I think of those who've gone.
Perhaps I too'd be better off.
Then . . . No! I'll soldier on.

I've tried the *oils* - the vitamins -
The cures both old and new.
You can't hold back the clock, they say,
I'm much afraid it's true.

I sense he's getting restless
That old man with his scythe -
I guess he thinks my time is up
I've had my share of life.

But if he thinks I'm east prey
That I'll just sit and wait -
He's got another think due him -
I've got a better date!

V E Egerton

THE SEEDS OF DUNKIRK

In the quiet of the night
when the waves are still,
the Heavenly Reaper stands
then gathers to Himself those fallen seeds,
which were scattered on yonder sands.

And the Reaper blessed those fallen seeds,
(He knew them all by name)
and planted each in some loved one's heart,
no matter from whence they came.

To the sands as well where those seeds lay
He gave His special blessing,
and the moving tides pass to and fro
each tiny grain caressing.

Then as the years move slowly by
and all the tears are shed,
the Dunkirk beaches will remain
a memorial to the dead.

Mike Coyle

AN AIR-RAID

The noise and smell with smoke abound
We panic dash like headless fowl,
As ululating siren warnings sound
Telling all to 'run and heed my howl.'

The angry air both terrified and torn,
As unexpected death in pain rains down
And pushes with contemptuous scorn
Our helpless homes in frightened town.

Excitement changed with horrors seen
To chattering fear and rising gorge.
The crumbling house begins to lean
With heat and flame from Satan's forge.

At sounds of falling roof and walls
We cover heads and scream in dust
As lungs are filled and noise appalls
Death's deadly scythe swings low in lust.

Peter Muirhead

TENDER FEELINGS

A reminiscing thought,
Of four grieving hearts,
Dad waves his red beret
As the train gave a blast.

His silver bright wings,
Like a shining bright light,
Through hazy smoke clouds,
Like a star shining bright.

Steam engine puffing,
Belching fresh smoke,
Children are waving,
The train travels home.

Exciting taut feelings,
Their Dad has come home,
Feelings so tender
With lumps in their throats.

Tears of joy, to have and to hold.
With pleasant held thoughts,
Their dreams for a lifetime,
They're going to hold.

A joy of joys,
To have Dad come home,
To hold us so tender,
Till we part once more.

A picture remembered,
From long, long ago,
The feeling still tender,
Of that day Dad left home.

Norrie Hill

THE CORPORAL

When I joined,
we didn't need no number -
we all . . . knew each other.

But I wants you,
to know your number -
cherish it . . . and when I asks,

Barks it out like you're proud of it.
Now then, what's your number lad?

> One-double-four-six
> two-five-three-seven, Sir.

That's right . . . but you don't sir me.
I'm a Corporal. You don't sir sarnts,
only sar-majors, an' officers, see.

You call me, Corporal.
Corporal means body, and
that's what we are - the body of the Army.

Sergeants are all very well, an' necessary,
but don't you ever forget that it's us
Corporals, as is the body of the Army.

What are we then?

'Corporals are the body of the army, Corporal.'

Good lad, young

> One-double-four-six
> two-five-three-seven.

Colin McIntyre

EVENING DEPARTURE

Tonight I watched the setting sun
Sink low on Arran Isle
I watched the day till it was done
Till all its light had gone, and while
It passed, I sipped and scented wine
Of fragrant, heather-laden air;
Sweet draughts of purest joy were mine
As I stood watching there.

To westward, 'gainst the crimson sky
The rugged peaks stood out
In purple silhouette, their high
Bare, rocky summits wreathed about
With ever-drifting wisps of cloud,
Reflecting tints of gold and red
As coming night prepared her shroud
And crying birds prepared for bed.

Along the shores of Lamlash Bay
Dwarfed by the heights above
The simple, clean white homesteads lay
Each one a witness to the love
And care with which its owner's pride
Was matched to Nature's grand design
In peace and harmony beside
The sea in front, the hills behind.

And as I looked out from the bridge
The other ships around
Began to move, as fading light
Made growing darkness more profound . . .
And colour went, save black and grey,
Except in daylight's last goodbye
Great streaks of crimson stretched away
To north, o'er land and sea, to Skye.

And then, the magic of the air
Was multiplied by sound
Across the darkened waters where
For all ships outward bound
There came the sound of Highland Pipes
Reflected from the fading shore . . .
Nostalgic, haunting Highland Pipes
As I returned to war.

Maxwell Bruce

THE VILLAGE GREEN

Busy birds, upon the wing
O'er the Village Green in spring;
    Chatter and song
    Flying among
The Elms of the Green.

Children make their way
To the Green to play;
    Their own right
    Their chief delight,
Games upon the Green.

In summer, men in white
Playing against the light;
    A century made,
    A wicket laid,
Upon the Village Green.

With summer nearly done
In the setting sun;
    Dancing leaves
    In the breeze,
Nature's carpet o'er the Green.

Where the old-timers meet
Frost upon the rustic seat;
    Mantle of snow
    Soon to go,
Leaving a greener Village Green.

Norman Hucker

A WORLD TOUR

In nineteen hundred and forty-three
A naval telegraphist I would be
So at seventeen years and several days
With a railway warrant I'm on my way

Pre-entry training, signal school
Months of study, worked like a fool
Drafted later, LCT
June the 5th to Normandy

On the beach at Arromanches
Lots of action, this is France
Back and forth with more supplies
A million parachutes fill the skies

Campaign over, back to Guz
Another draft waiting, off to Oz
Sydney, Singapore, Philippines too
Just another job to do

Saw Hiroshima, terrible sight
Full effect of the Allies' might
War now over, '45
So relieved to be still alive

Japanese prisoners at beck and call
Surprised to see them oh-so-small
Washing, cleaning, labouring too
Found them lots of work to do

Indefatigable, transport home
Aircraft carrier, not much chrome
Bombay, Gibraltar, rum a-plenty
Birthday here, today I'm twenty

Hostilities over, memories fade
The tour is finished, *expenses paid.*

John Conway

ROYAL CORPS OF SIGNALS 1943 - 1945

Special 'Y' Wing, was our address,
Five teleprinters and six tele-ops,
All under constant stress.

High Grade Cipher, together in fives,
Jumbled letters and figures galore,
Dominated our lives.

Speed and accuracy was our aim,
As many wireless messages
Monotonously came.

This GCHQ in Hertfordshire lay,
Three main pubs and Mental Hospital,
Beckoning us to stay.

'King William', pub of our choice,
With roaring fire and musical sound,
We sang with heart and voice.

Then on at midnight, off at seven,
Freedom for thirty-six hours.
Such was manna from heaven.

Then on at seven and off at midnight,
Noon to seven and seven to noon,
Four shifts of sheer delight.

No more did I need to roam,
After Strathpeffer, Edinburgh and camp,
Swansea since is forever home.

Sadie Rogan

GREY GHOSTS

Old sailors dream about their past,
Memories that will always last,
Of happy days long long ago;
Of shipmates who were good and true,
Proud to wear their navy blue.

We may be old and past our prime,
At least we know, we served our time
On fearless ships of wood and steel;
The Royal Navy was our life,
Our home through times of peace and strife.

And we can talk about the Med,
Of battleships in line ahead,
And submarines down in the deep;
Of cruisers with their six inch guns,
Destroyers on torpedo runs.

Of sloops and frigates, smaller ships
With canteen messing, untold trips
Through angry seas that raged and boiled;
The ice, the snow, the red hot sun,
Tombola and a tot of rum.

And so I think about those days,
Of youth and manhood, and the way
I spent my time aboard those ships;
Great ships they were, I loved them dear,
And in my dreams they still appear.

I see them now, my ships of war,
Riding on waves far from the shore,
Shiny Sheffield, Dido and Strule,
Ramillies, Crossbow and Delhi,
Haunting grey ghosts of years gone by.

F Collett

VETERANS OF VICTORY

A letter dropped through my letter box,
On what was my thirtieth birthday,
But, it was my calling up papers,
To sign on for His Majesty's Army.

The unit I would be joining
Was stationed in Oldham, Lancs,
A Sergeant was there to welcome me
And introduced me to the ranks.

After being kitted out came training
Then off to Northern Ireland
Where aerodromes were badly needed,
In case of a sudden last stand -

After one year we came back to England
To prepare for the great invasion
We had to play an important part
Normandy, being our destination.

We landed, soaked through at Arrowmanches
Which was a sandy seaside resort,
And helped construct Mulberry Harbour
Which proved a vital landing seaport,

Then to press onward was the watchword,
To help our comrades in battle
We passed on the roads piles of wreckage,
And in the fields were many dead cattle.

We travelled through France to Belgium
Then on to Holland and Germany.
Where we came under a hail of fire,
And tremendous activity.

Shells, shrapnel and bullets were flying,
Buzz bombs roaring through the air,
We were in a difficult situation
With danger lurking everywhere.

But the Germans were at last defeated
Finally meeting their Waterloo,
Now it becomes a part of past history
As all great events usually do.

Horatio Thomas Jenkins

UNTITLED

At a darkened London station, a crowded troop train stood,
we were en-route for Ireland, or so we understood.
All thro' the night we travelled not knowing where we were,
until we heard MP's call out, 'Come on you lot,' you're there.
But that, was only Scotland and still had far to go,
so why they searched our kit-bags, we simply, did not know.

We crossed the angry Irish Sea in the eerie light of dawn,
I wondered then, why I'd been born, was *this* my destiny?
On reaching Terra-Firma, in the guise of Belfast docks,
another train was waiting, to take us even further.
My friend along the side of me said, 'This is a cattle truck'
she opened up the other door and fell out on the track.

The *Sally Army* were at hand and gave us both some tea,
we staggered back along the line and continued on our journey.
At yet another station we telephoned HQ , a truck, a car,
a horse, no matter what, *but* no transport for an hour or two,
we weren't expecting you!

At 4 o'clock that afternoon
a tank arrived for us
Our nightmare journey, had not ended
it seemed without a fuss.

We trundled thro' the country lanes until abruptly stopped by 'Halt'
And 'Who goes there' advance, be recognised. We scarcely looked
quite human, as our heads appeared out top, the guards were
most astonished and then began to laugh -
We walked along like zombies, where *was* the blessed camp
But turning *one* more corner found, we had arrived at last.

Beryl J Dyer

DEBT TO THE FEW

Never so much has been owed to so few,
One of our greatest Statesmen claimed.
His reference was to the airmen in blue,
When victory in the air was gained.

The heart of our country was threatened by *Fritz*,
With aircraft in strength from the blue,
More carnage would have been left by the blitz,
But for the courage and deeds of the few.

There was Douglas, Peter, Johnnie and Stew,
Flying aircraft like *Spits* and the *Hurry*,
Pilots here named are but some of the few
Who caused Hitler's Armada to scurry.

Many fighters were lost and destroyed in the frays,
Countless men gave their lives it is true,
So it's right we remember those memorable days,
And our debt to the glorious few!

R W Curwen

THE BLOODY ORKNEYS 1941

The bloody town's a bloody mess,
No bloody trains, no bloody bus,
and no-one cares for bloody *us*,
      In bloody Orkneys.

The bloody roads are bloody bad,
The bloody folk are bloody mad,
They'll make the brightest bloody bad,
      In bloody Orkneys.

All bloody clouds and bloody rains,
No bloody curbs, no bloody drains,
The council's got no bloody brains,
      In bloody Orkneys.

Everything's so bloody dear,
A bloody bob for bloody beer,
And is it good? No bloody fear,
      In bloody Orkneys.

The bloody flicks are bloody old,
The bloody seats are always sold,
You can't get in for bloody gold,
      In bloody Orkneys.

The bloody dances make you smile,
The bloody band is bloody vile,
It only cramps your bloody style,
      In bloody Orkneys.

No bloody sports, no bloody games,
No bloody fun, no bloody dames,
Won't even give their bloody names,
      In bloody Orkneys.

Best bloody place is bloody bed,
With bloody ice on your bloody head,
You might as well be bloody dead,
As in the bloody Orkneys.

Cyril Henry Jordan

EARNEST BEVIN BOY

Anonymous civilian,
With water and mid-morning snap,
Waits dawn's first bus at Yarborough.
Destination colliery.

At end of yawning, sleepy ride
Dons helmet, boots and working gear.
When lamp collected, readily
Joins shuffling queue for pocket frisk.

Deep shaft descent in darkened cage
To subterranean working place.
Which road today? Which Deputy
To put the fear of God in me?

Long lines of rumbling, loaded tubs
Speed surface-bound along their way.
Crashes. Smashes. Spilled coal on floor.
Hot and sweaty. Fingers blistered.

No clocks down here. Silent. Eerie.
When instinct tells of time for home
From all points flickering light converge.
Bright sunlight dazzles tired eyes.

Hurried shower. Clean and tidy.
Back by bus to room in lodgings.
Tea. Forget those aching muscles.
Go for walk. Fresh air's a wonder.

I might have worn a uniform
And served with rare distinction,
But I like to think I did my bit
On morning shifts down Bentley Pit.

Stanley Longbottom

AN ODE TO ANN

Lonely beats the silent heart
Since the time we came to part
But cry you not my Darling Ann
It's all a part of God's own plan

Day up in the heaven's high
I can hear your lonely sigh.
But be brave my lovely one
For the time must surely come

When God Almighty he will say
Enough is enough for those who pray
Be it by night or in the day
He will answer 'What you may.'

His love and patience he bestows
On those who's left here in the glow.
When he sees fit He will raise you high
To join your lonely heart, By By By By.

L W Haynes

NORMANDY

Khaki clad we lie in wait,
Close by the embattled Norman shore.
Each man conscious of his fate,
To weave a tapestry of war -
      In Normandy.

Soon the evil roar of a thousand guns,
Defiles the summer sky,
And fate decides which of it's sons,
Will be the next to die -
      In Normandy.

Proud citizens of France with loyal heart,
Face the Hell of conflict loosened from it's chain,
As steadfast families play their lonely part,
To suffer death or misery and pain -
      In Normandy.

No 'Redcoat' tale of glory here we tell,
Where every yard of 'Bocage' takes its toll,
The thrill of action soon loses all its spell,
And war seals horror in our soul -
      In Normandy.

Then fear takes second place to pride,
As tired, our mighty armies pause,
Before we all move up for the next assault,
In our noble fight for peace and freedom's cause,
      In Normandy, 1944.

Dave Edwards

113

THOSE WARTIME DAYS

Declaration of war brought change we could not imagine,
All able men were recruited for serving.
To battle they were sent, in lands far and foreign,
Leaving families behind, to keep the home fires burning.

Metal for armaments compulsory collected,
Iron railings for weapons, saucepans confiscated.
Blackout enforced to shield us from bombers
Hooded lights, rationed petrol, and rationed groceries.

The call came for women to serve in armed forces,
Land Army, Nursing or Munition Factories.
To a sprawling Arsenal came my call to serve,
Filling detonators, and fuses, which took some nerve.

We worked in three shifts, all very unsocial,
And travelled in buses which we pushed when reluctant.
To trains we graduated, which were not much better,
Our singing made light of discomfort, so, no matter.

Contraband searches for things which caused friction,
Flameproof clothing, shoes rigid, and hat like porkpie,
Made us roar with laughter when the size was not right.
No comfort or style, no elegance in sight.

Rest breaks in canteen for tea and lunches,
Music while you work blared above chatting voices.
Good friendships were formed, a lifetime to last,
Support for each other through times happy or sad.

How different today, just fifty years on,
Life much more carefree for most of our young.
We suffered the days with pride and fortitude,
We, *The Forgotten Army* deserve much gratitude.

Dorothy Garvan

THE AFTERMATH

Through the years they came a marching
Phantom soldiers of the past

Smeared and bloody, torn and grimy
How much longer can it last?

Was written on their faces, young bewildered souls
They went to meet their sorry fate, death their only goals

Peace came, but oh at what a price
A million broken hearts and homes

A world now filled with filth and vice

Five and twenty years had passed
and once again, grim relentless horror o'er us
All our hopes had been in vain

Forces stronger than all others compel us
Now to show our might

Sacrifice our men and money to the
Bitter end to fight

Wives and families widowed, orphaned, young love
Blighted as its dawn

Left alone forlorn forgotten
Can this feeling be reborn?

Shrouded at approaching nightfall
A mourning world awaits her fate

Will the peace for which we're waiting
Be the peace that came too late?

Not if we will stand united
Stick together 'til the end

Pull one way the crush the horror
Homes and families to defend

Then at last beloved country
Of whom poets sing in praise

Stand supreme free protected
Once more thy gracious head to raise.

Vicky Ray

ROYAL SIGNAL RECRUITS

There's a racecourse in the market town of Thirsk and, so they say
The coldest winds in Yorkshire howl around by night and day
And when the 'Brass Hats' saw it, it looked so cold and damp
They said t'would be an ideal place to site an Army Camp
So they moved in a squad of Signalmen to live around the course
And brought in wireless sets and keys to try to teach us Morse
The *set room* was the grandstand, where the winners once were
chosen
But all us Signallers could do was sit there and be frozen
Where once they hailed a winner and toasted with champagne
We had to do our training and march in pouring rain
The bars they all stood empty where they drank the local ale
But aren't we all just grateful that we lived to tell the tale.

Robert W Smith

117

A CHILD OF THE WAR

Oh, haunting memories,
Bitter-sweet and flooding back
Of childhood days in wartime years,
Unlocking the past with provocative tears
And yet, the long, sunshine hours
Amid the Archfields and orchard bowers,
Bring jubilant, childish dreams to mind
Of a tomboy, eagerly, jar in hand
Setting forth with brothers so kind
Minnows to seek in a potholed land.

Cow-slipped meadows of my youth,
Gnarled old trees so joyously climbed,
Yet shrapnel had fallen all around
Amid the hideous whine of bombs to ground.
One small child remembers still
The thrumming roar of planes - they kill!
Be quick and run for cover,
Never heed the woodlands bright,
For you may never see another
Childhood day or untroubled night.

Such golden, crowded, halcyon days,
In tangled undergrowth we ran,
Sister and brothers searching for joy,
Minds in turmoil, girl and boy,
Picking berries mid dog-rosed field
But never a church bell ever pealed!
Hearts in mouth, nerves a-jangle,
Listening for tell-tale jarring whine,
Another raid, untimely wrangle
As man to man their wits combine.

Six, long, child-scarred years,
A father's absence bravely borne,
We three emerged, alive and well
To await his return, our tales to tell
Of woodland haunts and minnow ponds,
Of childhood trysts mid nature's fronds,
A little girl to womanhood grown
As Coventry, then London burned,
Two lads emerged, their boyhood flown
And childish innocence never returned.

Julia Eva Yeardye

MEMORIES

I have memories of that dreadful time
We went through during the war
How can I put them all in rhyme?
Let us hope there will be no more.

I worked so hard during night and day
A telephonist in the heart of London
Yet still we laughed come what may
But felt we were in a dungeon.

One day a bomb dropped in *the well*
Our building shook and our hearts stood still
But we lived thank God the tale to tell
Or worries, yes, we had our fill.

The fire bombs fell from out the sky
And the firemen aimed their hoses
They cheered us up and aimed them high
But life was not a *bed of roses*.

The Doodle Bugs came and then the *V's*
One fell in the river close by,
Hitler did not get us on our knees
But for the people gone I could cry.

Peace arrived at last thank God
The World gave one big sigh,
We hoped that all that now was past
And no more would have to die.

We picked ourselves up and carried on
Trying to rebuild our lives again
Our thoughts always with those now gone
Their sacrifice was not in vain!

Pat Fleming

WORLD WAR 2 MEMOIR

Burning cordite,
marching feet,
the scream of sirens.
How well I remember the tension of those
invasion hours.
D Day Portsmouth 1944.

All through the night
and long into the day
came the steady thud of marching men,
the swell of a calm sea as our armadas
nosed their way to the French coast.

What indomitable spirit inspires men
to go to war with a smile and a song?

Recollections of
Take Me Back To Dear Old Blighty
and *Land of Hope and Glory* as
the thronging landing crafts moved forward,
forward to victory by the fruits of
selflessness, devotion to duty,
and the fighting prowess of a truly
great people and of an even greater country.

Rita Brisk

UNTITLED

Off on a train, away from home
To a factory making planes for the war,
So scared, so young, a London lass,
Never away from my home before.

Put into digs with strangers too,
I cried and sobbed like a babe,
I wanted my mum to comfort me,
But the roots of the new life were laid.

Next day to the factory so big and cold,
I felt so alone and afraid,
But I met another London girl,
And in no time a friendship was made.

Three years passed by, I had settled down,
Then, it was back to London for me,
So many friends to leave behind,
But I had helped make Britain free.

E M Pace

HYMN FOR OUR FIGHTING MEN

Our men who left our shores to fight,
  Over the mighty sea,
O keep them ever in thy care,
  They fight for liberty.

Protect our men in jungles vast,
  To them Thy presence show;
O guide them, lift them, light them on,
  For Thee, they pray to know.

The men who rule the raging sea,
  Who fight its cruel blow,
O lay the mantle of Thy care,
  Round them and those below.

For men who sweep Thy heavens abroad
  Need all Thy love and care;
Protect them through long flights of hell,
  Be always with them there.

O Lord forget not folks at home,
  Who stand and never flinch,
Their thoughts are ever with our men,
  Who conquer inch by inch.

And so for each and all we pray;
  Let them not fight in vain;
O let the spark of peace for all,
  Be kindled to a flame.

E M Driver

A TRIBUTE TO OUR WARTIME BUSES

Buses, buses everywhere.
We see them here, we see them there
We see them everywhere.

Through snow and ice, rain and fog,
They did their best for us you know,
Your late today we know,
There was a raid last night you know.

Timetables to keep, tyres checked
Engines tune up, cleaners to make -
Them spick and span

All in all, they did their best and
Thank you all for travelling with us.

Irene Hitchin

THE FIRST OF THE FEW

I stood and gazed at the desolate field,
Where once silver planes had stood,
Poised and gleaming, ready for flight,
Prepared to face the enemies might.

Scramble! Scramble! Has gone out the cry,
Enemy planes have invaded our sky,
After them boys; on *A Wing and a Prayer*,
The Battle for Britain must be fought in the air,

Like airborne knights with silver wings,
They roared one by one to the sky,
Prepared to fight for freedom's life,
Though they themselves might die.

The planes of the enemy were like a dark cloud,
But our fighter pilots were brave and proud,
Proud of their heritage, proud of their land,
Well they knew theirs was a desperate stand.

For they were outnumbered, those brave boys in blue,
Compared to the enemy, they were indeed few,
But they were undaunted, well knowing the cost,
To their people, their country, should the battle be lost.

We prayed as we watched the dogfights on high
Wept for those shot down in flames from the sky
Courageously won was that battle of fame
The Battle of Britain the world knows the name.

I gazed once again at the old runway
Where now only the rabbits play
And thanked God for those boys in blue
Great Britain's Heroes, *The First of the Few*.

Christina Smith

THE RECRUIT

She worked in a factory,
Drove a bus
Worked on the land
Without any fuss
Fed the children on meagre rations
Hair in a turban, *factory fashion.*

Down the shelter
For the night.
Up in the morning
At first light.
Nose to the grindstone, shoulders back
A stiff upper lip, munitions to stack!

Dig for Victory,
Walls have ears,
Don't let the children
Know your fears.
Not just fathers won the war,
Mothers stayed home and evened the score.

Barbara Beddow

TRYING THEM ON

One for you, one for you,
And so on round the class.
Square-boxed, neat,
Cardboard-brown.
Ordinary.
But we were excited,
Presents were few.

The opening was the best bit.
Unsteady fingers unfolding flaps,
Feeling the concertina-ed rubber
Nestled in a rigid bed.

Lesson One.

Deep breath.
Chin in first.
Fit straps over back of head.

Lesson Two.

Check fit round cheeks and throat.
Ignore the tight pull
Across tender childhood skin
And Saturday-night-washed hair.

Lesson Three.

Forget stomach churning smells
Of hot, moist rubber.
Even if you are sick
Keep it on.

You were safe in your gas-mask.

Molly Price

ALONG THE LINES

The Labour Exchange said, 'Here's a job, if you can find a friend,
And reason is, you'll work with men, and snags there is no end,
So in due course, I settled in, as linesman's mate, no less,
Signal dept; was the job, and you didn't wear a dress,'
Up those ladders, oil and brush, to clean away the grime,
Miles of plod, from *arm to arm*, all along the line,
Rain and snow, from *box to box*, the tea was always waiting,
Then out again no lifts for us, the troops were busy fighting,
Waves from the *Boys*, all on the move, no time for romance or
flirting,
The fact I was married, made me toe the line, of that I was more than
certain;
My four years went by on *Great Western Railway*, of fun, and a job I
enjoyed,
The marriage lines proof of *GWR*, by them, I was proudly employed.

M Woodfield

BOMB ALLEY JUNE 1944

The wail begins - low, sinister and strong -
Now down the scale - then back to its note, high.
Moaning Minnie's warning - eerie, long,
The siren! The mother wakens with a sigh
And swiftly dons her coat.

The dim light's shaft reveals the sleeping child
Innocent life, marred by planes and raids and bombs.
It knows no fear, the mother's calm face, mild,
Guards her heart's anguish, but for peace she longs.
Her hair is turning white.

The limping father clutches child and bag
Filled with saved rations, sweets and bottled tea
Four minutes now - the only time they have
To leave the house and seek the shelter deep
Dug in Kent soil.

The Anderson's interior, dark, dank, cold, bare,
Swallows them in corrugated enclave
The drone of 'planes comes nearer - whistling fills the air -
The bombs dull, systematic thud, the adults quiet, brave -
The searchlights' glare.

Tin hat securely on, the father mounts the steps
To peer into the battle overhead. *Casualties! Houses are alight!*
No stay! The mother runs to hold his scarred legs.
As he limps off - away into the night -
A stranger noise is heard.

The chug, chug of a train - menacing, low,
A train overhead? Stretched over child, she hides her fear,
As huge blast levels six homes with one blow,
The shelter shudders - earth trickles from its roof - *It's all right, dear!*
She calms the wakened child.

Elizabeth Buckman

MEMORY OF BURMA

Beyond the Shwedagon Pagoda
With its golden Dome standing high
Glittering in the sun
Like a castle in the sky
Overlooking the city of Rangoon

With its swaying palm trees
And spicy smells
And the long winding and dusty roads
Leading through the Burma jungle
And the palm trees standing high
Shielding us from the scotching sun
And the tanning of our bodies

Disease in the jungle you cannot see
Vultures up above perch on the trees
Looking for their prey
Cutting through the the tangled jungle
And elephant grass growing tall
With the enemy you couldn't see

Through the night you can hear
The bull frog's croaking
Near the swamps.
In the silent of the night
And looking up at the stars
As we sleep at night.

G Mathew

HENS AND A BALANCER MEAL

Light Sussex crossed
With Rhode Island Red,
You all had an air
Of pride as you fed
On Balancer meal,
(Mixed by me at the sink).

You each had a name -
Millicent, Sue
Rhoda and Trudie -
But what could that do
When the time came
For young stock to oust you?

I am sad to remember
And brood on your fate
Which was to end up
As roast meat on a plate -
So did your rivals
On a different date.

But most I remember
With outrage the smell
(So often breathed, remembered too well)
Of Balancer meal
Mixed with kitchen scraps
That I stirred and I stirred.

J M Benians

MY MEMORIES OF WORLD WAR II

How can I forget the World War II?
Overnight all our lives soon changed its true.
Churchill's *News* on the radio reached us all,
Families would part when sons received their call
I lived with my folks in the country on a farm,
This peace would soon be shattered I felt with alarm!
Daughters, Mums and Dads, must all play a special part
Lovers would bid farewell, leaving many a broken heart.
Gas Masks, Ration Cards, food and clothing we must share,
Black Outs Air Raid Wardens - down a shelter we would prepare,
As each night our Sirens alerted us as they moaned and wailed,
We listened to the Luftwaffe as their dreaded hummm prevailed.
Daily local *News* we listened to and the raging *War* far away,
So offered my services as a Fire Warden, trained without delay.
My Grammar School had sadly closed, teachers and friends had
gone
Evacuated from Birmingham to country villages everyone!
Long bus rides I travelled, another school I shared,
Only half-a-day's schoolwork, taking homework to be prepared.
Later I left school and an insurance clerk became
Staff were being *Called Up*, many waited for their name.
Eventually I was called, as a Telephone Engineer trained . . .
Releasing a male engineer for the *War*, whilst I remained.
Travelling daily to the city often filled me with distress
Were trains or trams running? Busy firemen were clearing the mess.
Buzz bombs and Doodle Bugs *Gerry* sent these flying over
Our Barrage Balloons floated high giving RAF camps extra cover.
Huddled in cold shelters - with our guns booming in the night
Sleep would escape us waiting the *All Clear* and morning light.
I knitted socks for soldiers, wrote cheery letters too,
Sang and entertained the wounded - but, we were just a few!

Stella Bush-Payne

FOOTSTEPS

I was young, I was in love, happy and carefree.
Then, what had happened to many, happened to me.
Going to the station, managing a smiling goodbye,
The train steaming out, left alone, wondering why.

Don't worry, they said, each and everyone,
Six months from now, the war will be won.
I believed them, of course, but, in my heart,
Dreaded that short time we would be apart.

The postman's step. Would he pass the door?
The quiet certainty he'd stop, and then, no more.
Embarkation leave was a warning of how it would be,
But the waiting, the listening, was torture to me.

At last! At last! The postman's stopped.

As I flew down the stairs, I knew there would be
Dozens of letters, and each one for me.
No hint where he is, but, the joy, the joy,
He's alive and well and still my boy!

Not now daily letters, only now and again.
The months stretched to years - and then.
He's coming home - I can't believe it! When oh When?
Next month, he says, and we'll get married then.

Next month came, it was June forty-five,
They had surrendered, it was good to be alive.
As I listened for his step, which I knew so well
Thoughts and feelings overwhelmed me, too private to tell.

That loud step never came, the one I had known,
Wearily he walked, silent and alone;
I looked at his dear face, no longer young,
I looked at a man for whom life had begun.

Arms around each other, very little to say,
The five lonely years simply faded away,
Happier now than ever in life,
Tomorrow Thank God, we'd be man and wife.

Lilian Jane Price

UNTITLED

At seventeen I met a friend
At work in Lincoln's Inn.
The War carried on
And so did we -
Never giving in!

We typed all day
From nine till five,
And gave thanks
That we were still alive.

Despite the troubles,
We made the most of what we did -
Never losing heart.
At the Stationery Office we listed the names of all those killed:
To win the War we all did our part.

When the bombing began
We went to the basement
And counted heads on arrival.

This really was a case of survival.

Our backbone and our strength sprang from
The love we had at home.
So wonderful were our parents,
We did not care to roam.

Peaceful were the days - except for Hitler -
I still remember the beautiful Summer weather!
But the dark cold nights, and the deafening noise
Are etched in my mind forever.

We made a pact - if we were to survive -
To meet in Peacetime, somewhere bright and alive . . .
But life goes on, and we lost contact -
I wish so much that I could bring them all back.

Phyllis O'Connell

WAITING

The Imperials and the Underwoods are tapping
ATS and civilians alike
In a school where the military is mapping
And children are banished from sight.

The forms that this day I am sending
From wire basket the Major brought in
Are a pile of wound notices pending
And my keys are quicker than the pen.

Dear Mrs Smith, Jones or maybe Gray
Your husband brother or son
Has sustained a smashed useless vertebrae
At the end of a shell or a gun.

The hospital will send you some details
A pass will be sent to you soon
You will travel by bus or on rail
And the nurses will show you the room.

No erasures today are allowed from our crew
This paper is vellum and a special cream
Next of kin, *We regret to inform you*
Of this death and the end of someone's dream.

Personal Effects and the vision it brings
Where the bloodstained momentos come home.
Letters, wallets, watches and rings
Beloved trivia of those now left alone.

Dear Sir, is there nothing of his to pass on
Some treasured thing I may keep
To give from a father to his unseen son
By a mother who can only weep.

So one day will I too, get the letter I fear
From a fellow typist in some other town
A *Regret to inform you* headed with a crown
Re: My young husband of one treasured year.

M L Day

THOUGHTS OF AN EVACUEE

It's hard to get accustomed to a life so strange and new
It's hard to think I have to be so far away from you
To think that War has parted us, bringing so much sorrow
Oh to see the Cloak of War give rise to peace tomorrow.
I feel so strange living in this house I do not own
Cut off from the ones I love and seem terribly alone
All the time I'm thinking of the home we made together
Back in dear old London town - don't say it's gone forever.
Here I have been evacuated with our son so small
He knows not of this awful war or why we're here at all
But everytime he's put to bed and says his childish prayer
He asks the Lord to bless you and look after you with care.
Is it possible my dear, that we'll be together soon
Or will my dreams of happiness fade slowly with the moon?
If you could only be with me and soothe my broken heart
Life would be so much easier until death do us part.
But it's no use wishing for these things which cannot be
I must only hope and pray that our son will be more free
So that when he grows much older he will not have to fight
And risk his life for enemies who wish to show their might.
So I'll relax once more dear and be happy if I can
Trying not to think of War but of my beloved man
Who is out to crush the enemy and their so-called power
May the Lord be on his side every minute of the hour.

Marie Shapiro

THE OLD SCHOOL

Once again we meet to play, our annual game of darts.
None of us are experts - only at making tarts.
We do enjoy our visit. It's so friendly - we feel we belong.

Win or lose - doesn't matter. At the end we'll join in song.
We like coming to the old school. It reminds us of times long past.
Our memories are refreshed, as our minds way back are cast.

I can remember when this school was crowded,
With miner's daughters and sons.
And when they up and left girls made ammunitions
And boys learned to fire guns.
We were a tight knit community then,
And knew all our neighbours - and all the Gen.

Our *Ladies Clubs* do keep us in touch.
Reminding us we still belong to a community, and that means so
much.
I must congratulate *Maescynew* on the tremendous progress they've
made.
Since they began their *Ladies Club* and quickly reached top grade.

Now tonight we'll play our friendly game,
So darts at the ready - now - steady friend and foe.
Off you go. Mr Hitler you'll soon be on the run.
When all our good good deeds are won.

Muriel Davies

AND SO I SERVED

Split shift! what's a split shift - I asked;
Oh! You mean working all hours?
One week in three was their reply -
Don't seem too bad to me, I'll give it a go I said.
Always did fancy myself in *A Uniform*!
So placing my peak cap partly 'pon my head -
Navy divided skirt - for decency -
Jacket with shiny buttons, money bag slung to right side,
Ticket puncher resting upon my left hip -
I'm ready and off.
'One ring on the bell for stop, two for go!' -
Said my driver, - 'I'll remember! I replied.
'Fares please!' right money would help Sir -
Not yet having developed sea legs -
I swayed from side to side;
Wish I'd joined the Wrens now I sighed - still -
I'd rather be bus sick than sea sick 'Gosh -
We've passed *What Stop Did You Say* -
Where you wanted to get off!' Well it's only twenty yards back.
And as my first shift ends; my only consolation is -
That I've filled a breach, and enabled a man -
To go to war, whether he *wanted to or not.*
So I served, - never ever did charge a fare -
For any man in uniform; Army, Navy, Airforce -
This ride's on me, I said.
Sirens, smoke screens, blackouts, bombs, Vera Lynn -
But we won - didn't we?

Glenys Tarr

140

THE VOLUNTEERS

Sirens wailing, scurrying feet
Sleepy children dragged from sleep.
Firewatchers straining weary eyes
Searchlights sweeping cities skies.

Canteen helpers passing out tea
The streets are walked by the ARP.
The strident sound of the ambulance bell
The whine and whistle as the bombs fell

Fire engines roaring down the street
Faces burning from intense heat
Incendiary bombs have done their worst
Gas and water mains have burst

Dad's Army trained and ready to fight
Underground sleepers emerge with daylight
All anxiously watch and hope for good news
As they take their place once more in the queues.

Comforts for troops as the needles click
This one for Joe, that one for Mick
Ingenious menus, make do and mend
Salvage to save, letters to send.

Husbands, fathers, sons, have gone.
But day after day they carry on.
Turning out much needed planes and tanks
To win the war, will be their thanks.

E M Clowes

GERRY, POSTED MISSING

Some friends come home, and I have come
Back to a life we left when we were twenty,
There's little now where gaiety and laughter
Shone in some eyes that now are closed forever,
And a long six years have passed, a wintry youth
Has vanished in the darkness of our time.

I cannot say come stroll with us tomorrow
Into the sunshine of a later day, no, no,
Not you, who would enjoy the singing hours,
The promise that your future couldn't keep;
Those days we had, those golden hours of play
Are distant now, and games that opened well
Have been suspended by untimely death.

I saw you last in nineteen forty-one,
Where are you now, for no-one knows
Or even will, but I'm still waiting here
To tell you of a thought that's steeped in tears,
For if you could return to view these years
You'd know the sorrow as we look in vain
For wife and family you might have had.

If in the quiet of your silent night
You see these words, then know it now,
I think of you though years have gone,
And it seems so long ago when we were twenty.

G House

KATRINA

Will you live to be a babushka (granny).
On that land you once worked upon?
Will you get the chance to hear once again
How quiet flows Sholokov's Don?
Will you once more put on your gay costume
And whirl to a lively tune?
Will your lover sing of your Black Eyes
'Neath the birch tree kissed by the moon?

Yes I saw the Ukrainian women
Heard them sing in a soft minor key
There's no news from your homeland Katrina
But sometimes there's a letter for me.
Your towns are now fear tortured ghettos
Your villages ashes and mud
As the front rumbles nearer Katrina
Must we too disappear in its flood?

Will they give you a Birkenau shower
Where you're bathed in a toxic haze?
Where mass extinction by Zyklon B gas.
Is the most economic of ways.
Katrina I leave in the hour
What we share is uncertainty.
Many Auswitz like butchers will swing I've no doubt.
But others will get off scot free.

Dick Doyle

WARTIME JOURNEY

Mailbags on trolleys, parcels in piles,
Milk churns awaiting
Bicycles gleaming,
Trees wrapped in bags next to
Dogs tied with labels,
Pigeons in baskets talking of freedom,
Mysterious packages bound up with straw,
Fragile or urgent.

Kitbags in heaps
With name, rank and number,
Bound for secret destinations,
Three badge sailors
Jostling with hammocks,
Airmen in greatcoats, squadies on leave,
Waffs, Wrens and Wracs
All dreaming of home.

The echoing station
Blacked out and nameless,
Winding down tunnels
Of dark platforms curving,
Smelling of oil and gossamer steam.
In the all night buffet,
Pushing and heaving,
Two teas and a wad, please
But bring your own cups.

Harry Stevenson

TRAINING CENTRE BLUES

What a naive bunch we were
   Arriving at Training Centre,
Those poster girls of ATS
   Showed *glamour*, only to lure.

But in the next few weeks we found,
   As on our beds we lay,
Inoculations and blanket rash
   No *glamour* at all around.

Drilling all day on the barrack square,
   Wasn't our sort of fun
With uniforms not quite our size
   So little *glamour* to share.

Our beds were *biscuits* made of straw
   Pyjamas were far too large
And quite unmentionable underwear
   Glamour was just a guffaw.

The food was more than one could bear,
   Cold porridge all full of lumps
Stodgy puddings, helped down with jam
   Glamour became so rare.

Please take us back to Civvy Street,
   Became the plaintive cry,
We're overweight and underpaid
   Glamour? We can't compete!

But even, as recruits so raw,
   We all had signed the Pledge,
To fight for King and Country,
   And *glamour* won't win a war.

Rowena L Argent

I REMEMBER!

I remember well the day you said goodbye.
I was so proud of you, you didn't even cry.
We said so many trivial things to pass away the time
Some of them ridiculous, some of them sublime.

I remember well, as we were standing there,
I saw the love light in your eyes, the sunlight in your hair.
The clock was crying out *It's almost time for you to part.*
And then the whistle shrieked *Come on lets make a start*!

I remember well that last embrace - so dear,
I know your lip was trembling - I saw that hidden tear.
Then at the carriage window we hadn't very much to say,
But remember, I'm remembering you 'till I come back that way.

Arnold G Bishop

MEMORY MONTAGE

Sorting the strands of a tapestry
That took six years to weave,
Most of us lost our youth at that time
The sacrifice hard to believe.
Blackouts and gas masks and windows taped.
Sand bags at every entrance.
No lights on trains through no name stations.
Theatres with no night performance.
The next year war started in earnest,
Countries fell till we stood alone.
The casualty lists started growing,
And the LDV army was born.
The women were being called up as well,
And those who were reserved,
Worked in offices, factories, hospitals,
In a quieter way - served.
Food rationing now was a fact of life.
Clothes coupons. Make do and mend.
Dried eggs. Woolton Pie and American spam.
And a new phrase was heard . . . Lease Lend.
There were deaths in all families. Prisoners of war.
A wedding without a white gown.
Giving birth in an air raid without any light.
Leaving home for an alien town.
VE day arrived and the street lights switched on.
Nations now counting the cost.
War finally ended with atoms unleashed,
The world's age of innocence - lost.

Ida Shewan

STILL DANCING

Why, oh why should they have to fight?
An announcement, those captured, missing and died.
Yes, I had a good time last night.
Don't mention the tears we had to hide.

Working in East Anglia during the war years,
There were many opportunities to dance;
Inspite of all our worries and fears,
We enjoyed ourselves given the chance.

Visiting the area again in 1992,
My mind went back to fifty years ago;
This was a case of déjà vu,
From Land Army days toiling with my hoe.

When I returned home to Hatfield,
At the local community centre after dinner;
Checking notices a celebration dance appealed,
Gee! this special outing sure is a winner.

An American Connection Weekend in Braintree,
With many ceremonies and events taking place;
Including something I wanted to see,
The all women band and Ivy Benson's face.

A welcoming speech for the returning Yanks,
Then dancing with the jitterbug and jive;
An American veteran expressing his thanks.
It made us feel glad to be alive.

Why, oh why should they have to fight?
Now it seemed they were by our side.
Yes, I had a good time last night.
Don't mention the tears we had to hide.

P V Robbie

THE MEN ENGLAND FORGOT

Far away across the ocean,
  Lies a land so fair and sweet,
Winding hills and valleys,
  With the houses small and neat,
Once a land so free and easy,
  Home of England's fighting sons,
Now the home of Poles and Frenchmen,
  Yanks, and those Canadians.

In its towns and country lanes,
  Where we used to love to walk,
You can see them swank and swagger,
  Using brave and boasting talk.
What they'll do when they get started,
  How they'll finish off the war,
What they're going to do to Jerry,
  But we've heard all that before!

In the meantime, in the desert,
  Far from sweethearts, and their wives,
Britain's tough and hardened heroes,
  Fight like madmen for their lives,
Tired and thirsty, scorched and blistered,
  Blinded by the driving sand,
Half forgotten by their loved ones,
  In this God forsaken land.

See them waiting every morning,
  For their highly treasured mail,
Knowing well that they will find it
  Once again, the same old tale.
Oh how often we have seen it,
  Watched that agonising face,
Something in that letter tells him,
  Someone else is in his place.

Can we curse the rank outsider?
  Can we give him all the blame?
Or should those impatient women,
  Hang their guilty heads in shame?
We must not blame everybody,
  Just those few unfaithful ones,
In a way, they're worse than Jerry,
  Worse than all those German guns.

Remember then you wives and sweethearts,
  When you feel you cannot wait,
What has your man left to live for,
  When he finds he's lost his mate?
After all, you have England,
  And a friend to hold your hand,
But without you and our country,
  All he has left is blood and sand!

S V W Bentall

VE DAY

I was almost a teenager -
And remember the jubilation and crowds -
Grown-ups, normally so docile,
Lost their heads and seemed to go just wild!
Trumpets, drums, old saucepans and spoons,
Made a brilliant cacophony -
We ran down the High Street to watch this -
Not realising we were watching History!

Gradually the soldiers started returning -
Not all to the happy families they left -
Divorces for many were in the future -
But, for now, no-one seemed to want to look that far ahead.

Schools closed for the day.
There were Street Parties -
Mums baked with the last of their rations.
Yet, without the sophistication of today -
They produced a veritable banquet -
All handmade, with love, for that wonderful Day.

Now we would start to forget all the bad memories -
The bombings, the deaths and the rest -
Here was that New World they all went to fight for -
The New World that would put in the shade all the rest.

Years have gone by, and still I remember,
The days of the war and the losses.
Yet in these days of veritable plenty -
There seem to be so many people bearing personal Crosses!

Each day I give thanks for my Freedom -
Fought for by our army so long ago.
Thank you, each one, I am grateful -
Without your sacrifice I would not have seen
My children and grandchildren grow!

Janet Sarkar

THE LAST FAREWELL

They fly now in the sunshine
They're free above the clouds
Not for them the stony ground
A covering of shrouds.

Their spirits happy, roaming free,
Of their valour angels sing,
All companions there alongside,
Heaven's sunshine on their wings.

In our hearts they flew to glory,
And as the years unfold,
Ever in the tales of heroes,
Their story will be told.

Cry not for us tho' we are sad and low,
We have our friends around us here and so
Together we can rest now,
So mourn not when you know.

But when the flames of war
Are just a dying ember,
Use our peace well, and think of us,
That's all we ask, *remember!*

F J Hutchinson

FORGOTTEN

The sun came up in the east
Swift and savage, like a beast.
Slipping, silent through the spray
This was just another day.

But before the dawn had broke
Action stations - men awoke
Stumbling, swearing on their way
This was just another day.

Locked below decks, in the heat
Sweating, staring at their feet
Was the enemy far away?
This was just another day.

At our stations - we all stayed
Watching, waiting, and we prayed
This was just another day
Across the world, no longer fearing
Folks were laughing, crying, cheering
For all at home - the world was gay!
This was not another day!
Over the air - the news they'd send
V E Here - war's at its end.

But down below taut with fear
For us the enemy was near
For this was just another day.

E Hannaford

UNTITLED

At WVS I was, to the canteen
for early breakfast I must go.
To feed the troops on their way
a while to rest, a tummy to fill
Smiler, they called me, to cheer
them on their way.
The aerodrome I went to as well.
Wellington boots to guard me
against the mud and snow.
Hurry up Smiler, we're on our
way the bosh to fight till end of day.
Cheer up lads! Here I come
hot tea, to warm you up.
Food to keep you on the go.
Please return safe I love you so.

Jeanne Lede

YES, WE HAVE NO BANANAS

The doodlebugs are coming down,
The air-raid siren blares,
And all of us, except my dad
Are underneath our stairs.

My mum has got her gasmask on,
Goes nicely with her pinny!
And dad, who's in the ARP
Is busy, helping *Winnie!*

Dad has a helmet, black and white,
One day some shrapnel struck it,
He also has a stirrup pump,
Long shovel, and a bucket.

My dad is, tho' a modest chap,
A hero in our town,
He led some people down the lane,
And then their house fell down!

My mum is quite a hero, too,
Or so says dad, when eating,
What she can do with powdered egg
Would take a bit of beating!

'I'll be back' says dad to us,
'Don't worry have no fear'
He kisses mum, and then he adds
'And you make sure you're here!'

I've still got his old ration book,
The whistle that he had,
I've still got helmet, black and white
- I wish I had my dad!

Peter Davies

FORGOTTEN ARMY

We worked an 80 hour week
Despite so very little sleep.
A special treat of porridge oats
Cooked in water, served as groats
Small piece of bacon or dried egg
On half a slice of bread was spread
The other half - a piece of toast
Was all our breakfast meal could boast.
Then came 5 hours of hard drudge
(None of which we could dodge).
At last, a short break for our dinner
That *diet* helped us all get thinner!
We then worked on again till five
Two cups of tea helped us survive,
One slice of bread, and just one bun,
Then evening duties must be done.
First blackout shutters to be closed
Curtains drawn - no light exposed.
Quite soon the siren sounds again -
Is it a doodle-bug or plane?
An awful silence fills the house
All are as quiet as a mouse.
Then, thud, thud, a dreadful sound,
We asked 'How many folk are found?
So many casualties, we fear
For ambulances pass quite near,
Work done, a cup to calm us all
Then, weary into bed we fall,
But first, a prayer to God above -
'Please keep us safe and those we love.'

JM

THOSE DREADFUL YEARS OF WAR

The Youth of our land had joined the armed forces
So we, left at home, had to muster our resources
And by working together the entire British nation
Overcame all problems and much deprivation
We opened our homes to the evacuees
And made Woolton pies in our factories
We tilled the ground and milked the cows
Gathered the harvest and mucked out the sows
Darned our stockings, made do with old clothes
Dug potatoes from clamps until our fingers froze
Worked at producing arms and ammunitions
Tried to work miracles with the food in our kitchens
We knitted those long oily seaboot stockings
Woolly scarves, gloves and socks all necessary things
Through the blackout we would go to the voluntary canteens
Which catered for the Forces on rare off-duty evenings
In those dark anxious days of the Battle of Britain
When bombs were exploding, incendiaries falling
And doodlebugs droning their way to destruction
We just kept on working, praying and hoping
The valiant VADs and stalwart ARPs
When the sirens sounded, at their post they would be
Peace came at last on VE Day
No bombs were dropping that night
Instead we lit glorious bonfires
Symbols of freedom and light
Our thoughts were on those who would never return
As we stood round the glowing red embers
A poignant moment! For the Forgotten Army
Which we for evermore shall remember.

F M Dixon

A WIFE ALONE

I was a women with baby small, born after Chamberlin
gave the call, 'No war' He was four months old
when war began, then they took away my man
we were living in Croydon all alone, husband
in the RAF, seldom coming home, going to shelters
every night, the town with bombing and alight,
everyone was caring, sharing,
it takes a war to bring people together,
shoulder to shoulder, in all kinds of weather.

I took my young son to Somerset, in a vicarage
we did stay,
where the vicar had opened up his home,
to all who came his way,
there were Jews, Chinese, Catholic and C of E,
he took into his care, we were all much
safer there.

The war went on - our home was bombed
we lost everything we had,
my husband got compassionate leave,
we were very sad,
the war was over, we had nowhere to go
The Croydon Council offered us a hutment
This is where we went, my husband
Was in India a long way away.
It was very hard to start again, to get a home
together, cueing up was all I did,
in all kinds of weather, very little in the
shops for anyone to buy,
but with my tokens I had a try.

At last a little home again began to appear
for Bob was coming home again, after all those years,
We welcomed him with open arms, and many many tears,
But now we have been together for 57 years.

Emily Green

158

REFUGEES

The aspens shiver as the summer breeze
Drifts softly through the avenue of trees.
It ruffles plodding peasant womens' skirts,
Plays over chests, and under open shirts,
And tousles bobbing curls that frame the child
Who lolls at ease among the chattels piled.
The creaking farm cart trundles through the dust,
Wheels raising clouds, that settle like a crust
On sweating brow, and horses steaming flank:
None see on high the glint, the sudden bank,
Or hear the roar, the rattling, coughing spit ,
Shocked silence; then as fiends from the Pit,
The wailing scream of souls, doomed, damned and lost,
Where crumpled dolls lie sprawling, careless tossed,
With skirts awry, and shirts mere bloody rags:
Yet still the horse plods on, the cart still drags,
The sun still shines, dust hangs still in the air,
And still among the chattels, I see where
The curly head still lolls, with eyes that gaze
Unseeing at the aspen-filtered rays.

Leslie D Deal

FIGHTERS ALL JUST A MUM

Our backs all against the wall,
We rallied when Churchill gave a call,
Man, woman, child, all done their bit,
Through fire, blood, we held our grit.

Food was scarce, rationing had to be,
Life was precious we all had to agree,
Brave men fought battles every day,
Many lost, others struggled to keep enemy at bay.

We fought on, times were rough,
No good grumbling, we had to be tough,
Keeping this way, the end came in sight,
Victory at last won with our all our might.

G Davies

THE WOMEN'S LAND ARMY

When Adolf and his cronies
Made England sound the call to arms,
We joined the Women's Land Army
And went working on the farms.
We got into our milking jackets,
Green jerseys and dungarees;
We planted potatoes, hoed the weeds
And lumber jilled the trees.
We learned how to drive a tractor
In the bomb scarred fields of grain,
We sheared the sheep, fed the hens
As incendiaries fell like rain.
We found a love of growing things,
Learned how to milk a cow,
We mowed the meadows, raked the hay
Learned how to use a plough.
With our pampered day of plenty gone
We roughed it in the fields,
But our efforts were not wasted
When we harvested our yields.
We didn't fight with guns or bombs,
But with hoes and forks instead;
We really dug for victory
And kept our country fed.

Pamela Eckhardt

CIVIL DEFENCE MEMORIES OF WORLD WAR TWO

Do you remember Sunday nights at the *Kings*
And the night of a raid, when we all had to sing
The building vibrated with blast from the Hun,
And the band I remember was Bob Williamson.
Blackout, and torches, and stirrup pumps too,
Flour bags for tea towels, and home made bone stew;
Fire watch, and knitting, and letters to send,
To our boys overseas, and the make do and mend;
Gas masks and helmets, and pink Mickey Mouse,
The Wardens so helpful in checking each house;
Blankets, and dockets, and queues for our food,
Rations of sweets, and Black Market goods;
Candles, and craters, when bombs fell quite near;
Cocoa, and Oxo and watery beer;
Wellington boots, an old sweater, and socks,
Worn for three weeks without a good wash;
The spirit of friendliness then did abound,
And the barriers of class were not to be found;
The day it all ended brought sadness for some,
But the lessons we learned were indeed welcome.

Ruby Biggs

WE LIVED AS MOLES

Not under a smooth green sward but under a road
A grey road, soulless.
We had no teens.
We had no fear that our shelter may become a tomb.
Our dad was at the helm.
Above, the road desolate.
Below, laughter, camaraderie, compassion, but no fear.
We flowered, us young ones on moonlight.
Experts on clouds, bad weather, fog.
Experts on weather conditions that would bring the black bombers.
And the droning, constant droning.
How proud we were.
Never doubting all would be well.
With our dad at the helm.
The sweet sound of the all clear.
As the dawn broke.
We shook ourselves.
Back home to wash.
Off to work.
We had survived another night.
Laughter showed our hidden relief.
We could look ourselves in the face.
We were there.
Our pride remains to this day.
That we were . . .

Joan Eyles

BOYHOOD MEMORIES OF WORLD WAR TWO

Once I saw up in the sky
A German bomber flying high
And watched as all its bombs came down
A little distance out of town
Staverton was the place they fell
'The aerodrome' I heard folk tell.

Then one day in Nineteen Forty
I saw another German sortie
Having a dog fight right overhead
'One's been hit,' a spectator said
Vapour trails just filled the sky
Where they'd battled there on high
I think it was a Mess and Spit
Those pilots certainly had some grit
I really don't know who eventually won
But for me it was tremendous fun.

Food and sweets did still abound
But they had to be shared around
And so rationing came into being
And with the shop keeper agreeing
You could have some, quite a lot
If the coupons you had got
But these were very quickly spent
So some to the black market went
Spivs appeared who were very fly
They could provide, but the price was high
When caught they'd say, 'I'm very sorry
The goods fell off the back of a lorry.'
But usually by Bench decision
They were packed straight off to prison.

Harold Eley

FROM HELL

The morning was grey at Liverpool dock
We waited with buses' and trains
For the men coming home
From horror's unknown
We were shortly to learn - to our shame
That these who had suffered
Torture and pain
Were singing and happy to be on our train
Us medics were working
To comfort and plan
To return home - these brave men -
From the camps of Japan.

Eddie Sommers

THE EVACUEE

It started one September day
When I was five and couldn't say
'What's all the fuss about today'
'Why have I got to play . . .'

At filling up this pillow case
With teddy and what's the race
To line us up outside the base
Of Euston station - why this place?

Why am I here and where's my mum
This train is not a lot of fun
Why couldn't mum and daddy come
Evacuees we've all become.

New homes, new schools, new faces here
'Now deary dry that silly tear.
Your mummy will be coming near
Next week so cheer up, never fear.'

'You're six today so you can play
With Suzy's doll for just today
And you can use the baby pram
We're borrowed from her sister Pam.'

'Now just you kneel down by that chair
And in your jamas say a prayer
And ask God to take special care
Of London and all living there.'

F Masters

FURIOSO

When first we started touring we had
A fine robust morality squad.
These pious ladies undertook
To quell romance with but a look.
While they were about there'd never be
Wanton promiscuity.
This their proud boast, but sad to say
Love will always find a way.
They didn't know quite where to begin
With such an overabundance of sin,
And so they hurriedly bid adieu
Complete with all that spells virtue.

Mamie Williams

REMEMBER

I was but a kid of ten
When war began.
I never forgot the sirens
Or the droning of the planes.
The falling of the bombs.
These weren't my games.
My dad had to go to war.
Clad in his army suit.
To Italy and Africa, the Suez on route
An eighth army man, I recall so plain.
While mum went to work
For some cash, to help out.
I remember it well
The day our bomb came October it was,
Trapped in our shelter in London, I was.
For a cockney am I
Through and through
And Leyton was bombed
And like all England did
We lost mums and dads, grans and kids.
Friends of mine are buried deep
Neath soil of London fast asleep.
We never shall know
Where some went too.
When our bomb came down in '42.
But now a pensioner I can say
I too can remember
What price some did pay.

Florence Brice

THE FORGOTTEN ARMY (BURMA)

To see you once, to kiss your face.
To hold you in a sweet embrace.
To tell you how much I care.
And without you life is bare.
To sit and have you on my knee.
To really have you close to me.
Oh darling, will you ever know,
How much I miss you so.

Stan Smith

A WAR CHILD'S DEFIANCE

When the bombs were falling
I heard someone calling
From a blitzed building far away.
Children were a crying
Sirens gradually dying
As I struggled on through the fray.

Ambulances were hurrying
Fire engines scurrying
Along the roads at great speeds.
They do their job well
And Hitler can go to hell
If we do the job that Britain needs.

G A Beale

THE FORGOTTEN ARMY

Serving tea and cakes to soldiers,
In the Sally Ann canteen,
To some who were raw recruits
While others in action had been.

In Italy, Africa, Norway, France
What horrors of war they had seen
Brave soldiers who wore their berets
Of Khaki, black, red and green.

For me no foreign travel,
No medal of victory
One of the forgotten army
Serving soldiers with cups of tea.

C E Cannon

THE FORGOTTEN ARMY

Young girls were we my friends and I
Just seventeen plus no more
Our country needed us to help the men that were at war
In a factory hidden far from view
We laboured every day.
The tiny tubes that we did make
Released 'Bombs away'
We thought we heard the airmen's cry,
To his pilot as they flew
Another sortie was complete
Success to the boys in blue!

Barbara Turner

REFLECTIONS

Air raid sirens, blitz and bombs,
Women at home thinking of husbands and sons.
Telegrams arriving, people froze at their door.
We prayed to God, 'Oh! How many more?'
To King and Country loyal they remained
Even with sons in unknown graves.
The last all clear was a joy to behold,
We all sang together as the men came home.
There were tears and laughter, the atmosphere great.
We all had something to celebrate.
But the heroes lost in our hearts will stay
Especially on Armistice Day.

Freda Dickinson

THOUGHTS OF A SOLDIER IN THE FIRST WORLD WAR
DARK ISLE

The cock is crowing far away,
As the guns of war scorch the sky,
Some mothers son has gone to rest,
Carried home in body bag,
That I can hear another day,
Whispering for the dead now fell,
The enemy beast is on the run,
And all I see is the Dark Isle,
They tell me to toe-the-line,
For all intended purposes,
They tell me revenge is sweet,
And from where I stand,
I'm sure it is,
But I feel nothing for this fight,
Where truth goes unrecognised,
All I feel is the scars of hate,
And all I see is the Dark Isle,
The just shall sleep in paradise,
Free from the clutch of tyrants greed,
Where hunger pays the heavy price,
To the fallen Gods of wars machine,
For time is short and days are long
And passion swift the snipers aim,
A million faceless corpses at my feet,
And all I see is the Dark Isle.

Ian Towers

KIRKCALDY LADS AND LASSIES

My thoughts stray back
some sixty years.
I hear the ghostly feet,
as lads and lassies promenade
along our local streets.
Some stood in groups
and then passed on.
No cares did we display,
till that September, clouds of war
gathered on the braes.

Flowers of my youth in uniform,
marched with heads held high.
Now they lie in foreign graves,
or in the oceans died.
Sore hearts, in truth, they left behind.
They fought the years of war
(To give to us a world of hope
so we can walk our shores).

Again the National Right Wing Groups
raise their ugly heads.
To strike fear in the young and weak.
We must be strong, not led!
Or all the young men
of my youth
Who lie in foreign graves,
have died for *what!*
Or died for *nought!*
The world they died to save!

Jane Wallace

INFORMATION

We hope you have enjoyed reading this book - and that you will continue to enjoy it in the coming years.

If you like reading and writing poetry drop us a line, or give us a call, and we'll send you a free information pack.

Write to

Arrival Press Information
1-2 Wainman Road
Woodston
Peterborough
PE2 7BU.